Identity, Religion, and Values

Identity, Religion, and Values: Implications for Practitioners

C. Margaret Hall, Ph.D.
Georgetown University
Washington, DC

Taylor & Francis
Publishers since 1798

USA	Publishing Office:	Taylor & Francis 1101 Vermont Avenue, NW, Suite 200 Washington, DC 20005-3521 Tel: (202) 289-2174 Fax: (202) 289-3665
	Distribution Center:	Taylor & Francis 1900 Frost Road, Suite 101 Bristol, PA 19007-1598 Tel: (215) 785-5800 Fax: (215) 785-5515
UK		Taylor & Francis Ltd. 1 Gunpowder Square London EC4A 3DE Tel: 171 583 0490 Fax: 171 583 0581

IDENTITY, RELIGION, AND VALUES: Implications for Practitioners

1 2 3 4 5 6 7 8 9 0   B R B R   9 8 7 6

This book was set in Times Roman by Sandra F. Watts. The editors were Caroline Schweiter and Holly Seltzer. Cover design by Michelle Fleitz. Printing and binding by Braun-Brumfield, Inc.

A CIP catalog record for this book is available from the British Library.

∞ The paper in this publication meets the requirements of the ANSI Standard Z39.48-1984 (Permanence of Paper)

Library of Congress Cataloging-in-Publication Data

Hall, C. Margaret (Constance Margaret)
    Identity, religion, and values: implications for practitioners/
  C. Margaret Hall.
      p. cm.
    Includes bibliographical references

    1. Psychology, Religious. 2. Identification (Religion)
  3. Values. I. Title.
  BL53.H24 1996
  220'.1'9—dc20

                                 96-17628
                                    CIP

ISBN 1-56032-442-2 (case)
ISBN 1-56032-444-9 (paper)

Contents

Acknowledgments

Many family members, friends, and colleagues have influenced the ideas and strategies described in this book. In particular, my parents, who are from the north of England, taught me what it means to be a religious person in Anglican or Episcopalian terms, and my husband introduced me to Judaism. Later, my three daughters taught me more of what it really means to be Jewish. Because these different sets of religious values played such a strong role in the development of my identity and individual empowerment, I have consistently asked the question of how religious values affect clinical interventions and client progress throughout my research.

Over the years Murray Bowen, M.D., and Rabbi Edwin Friedman have showed me critical differences between family processes and the influence of religious beliefs. Similarly, David Ruth, Ph.D., has helped me to appreciate the salience of sacred or secular belief systems for most people, and Gillian Lindt, Ph.D., has helped me to appreciate the roles religion plays in social change. More recently, Rabbi Joseph Weinberg, Rev. Hilda Paucitis, and Jane Kopp, Ph.D., have taught me some in-depth complex dimensions of religious history, as well as principles for practicing prayer, meditation, and spirituality in everyday life. Roberta Gilbert, M.D., has kept my attention on the dynamics of relationships and family systems, as well as the influence of spirit.

My colleagues at Georgetown University give me continuing opportunities to teach courses in comparative religion, such as "Identity and Religion" and "Religion and Values in Modern Society." I also participate in ongoing faculty discussions about the Jesuit nature of Georgetown University and the impact this particular historical religious identity has on the quality of education at Georgetown. With regard to a more practical level of day-to-day work, I am particulary grateful for the administrative assistance of Leslie Byers and Carol Gangnath.

Colleagues from the Georgetown Family Center, the Sociological Practice Association, and the Sociological Practice Section of the American Sociological Association helped me to hone my clinical skills, and have provided forums for continuing discussions and debates about clinical strategies and results. These networks offer meaningful support, ongoing inspiration, and challenges to make pioneering contributions in clinical research.

However, perhaps most of my thanks are due to the clients who have worked with me for varying lengths of time, as well as for different purposes, over the past 25 years. I have learned much from their efforts to articulate and make their own value choices, and from the wide range of clinical interventions used to bring about constructive behavior changes. Many effective challenges to the status quo are made through clinical interventions, and much solid evidence suggests that they can improve the quality of clients' lives significantly.

Without the expert guidance of Elaine Pirrone, Senior Acquisitions Editor at Taylor & Francis, *Identity, Religion, and Values* would not have its current substance and form. Her timely written comments and discussions clarified my thinking and helped me to develop my major themes. Bernadette Capelle, Development Editor at Taylor & Francis, added valuable insight throughout the development of the project. Holly Seltzer, Production Editor at Taylor & Francis, worked hard to refine my written words in bringing this book to fruition.

Preface

Identity, Religion, and Values: Implications for Practitioners is a handbook for clinicians and practitioners such as psychologists, social workers, clinical sociologists, health and mental health professionals, marriage and family therapists, counselors, and psychiatrists. Students in these professional fields will also benefit from its broad approach to clinical interventions and clinical applications, which emphasizes the roles of religious beliefs and values in interpersonal behavior and society (Hall, 1986a, 1991; James, 1969; Progoff, 1985).

This book is based on 25 years of clinical research and practice. It focuses on religion and spirituality as serious topics of concern for clinicians, who ostensibly intervene in clients' lives to improve their functioning and living situations.

Although some clinical research already points the significance of religion for quality of life issues, these studies have tended to be based primarily on intrapsychic or interpersonal data. In other words, to the extent that clinicians have considered religion and spirituality strong influences in defining patterns of behavior, these influences have been relatively compartmentalized and restricted to interpersonal milieus, rather than viewed within broad social contexts.

This book presents religion and spirituality as modes of social belonging and as critical sources for value choices. As individuals make value choices, they become increasingly connected with the religious or spiritual sources of those values, ultimately being more social in their orientation and concerns. Thus, by selecting religious or spiritual values as their own, clients can strengthen their identification with specific groups in society, as well as clarify which goals, ideals, and objectives they want to accomplish.

In its role as a handbook for clinicians, this book suggests ways in which such a broad frame of reference can help to strengthen the theoretical orientations, and therefore the effectiveness, of clinicians in their work with clients. Identity empowerment theory describes both micro- and macrosociological forces as powerful influences on behavior and the formation of belief systems. It is only when either clinicians or clients are sufficiently autonomous, however, that they can realize and realistically assess these influences, as well as act deliberately to take charge of their own cultivation of social values.

Another reason that it is important to understand that religion and spirituality are vital influences on clinical interventions is that these kinds of values are powerful motivators of behavior. Because of the emotional and moral intensity of specific religious or spiritual values, they can provide clients with purposes and directions that go beyond any short- or long-term clinical intervention. If clinicians are in the business of transforming lives for the better, these are without a doubt serious concerns, which merit close scrutiny.

In this book, the first eight sections of Chapter 2, and the first seven sections of Chapters 3 through 12, outline a range of important substantive issues that have been documented as having strong influence on identity and religion or belief systems (Appleyard, 1993; Ashbrook, 1993; Hechter, Nadel, & Michod, 1993; Mead, 1934). These themes are valuable topics for discussions in clinical sessions, and are also used as bases and perspectives for formulating clinical strategies (Glassner & Freedman, 1979).

C. Margaret Hall

Chapter 1

Introduction

As mentioned in the preface, this book is meant to be a handbook for clinicians and practitioners as well as a tool for students. Its central focus is how individuals and groups strengthen their identities through making deliberate value choices (Hall, 1990a). This main theme is illustrated by the substantive, structural, and process concerns about identity and religion that predictably arise when clinicians empower individuals or groups through strengthening the effectiveness of their interaction within and among communities (Glassner & Freedman, 1979). For example, marital discord can be clarified and reduced by orienting partners to their respective priorities and belief systems. Ideally, these kinds of clinical interventions eventually culminate in both individual and social benefits (Randour, 1993; Wuthnow, 1991).

This book addresses deep emotional aspects of identity and their relationships to religious and spiritual beliefs (Bowen, 1978). For example, individual assumptions about human nature are inextricably tied to beliefs about the universe. Furthermore, depth of religious commitment has been thought of as an aspect of primordial being (Tillich, 1952). Individuality, families, gender, social class, culture, and society are discussed as both starting points and contexts for understanding correlations between identity and religion (Hall, 1981), because everyday interaction and world views have significant influences on quality of life (Smith, 1987; Strunk, 1979). Related topics, such as ways in which religions define responsibilities and influence social change (Weber, 1958), are also discussed.

This book outlines new additions to clinical knowledge through specifying key generalizations, propositions, and value choices associated with identity and religious or spiritual belief systems and practices. For example, a social systems view of self is seen as critical to understanding and changing the self. This knowledge invites the construction of new approaches to clinical interventions, as well as to new ways to facilitate and promote individual or social changes (Kaufman, 1993). Widely shared survival or fulfillment concerns—such as the beliefs in supernatural powers reflected in diverse religions—are analyzed and discussed, and ultimately incorporated into clinical intervention techniques (Randour, 1993).

DATABASES

One of the most significant sources of empirical data for this book is a compilation of clients' answers to series of open-ended questions from clinical and research interviews. The author has conducted more than 1,000 clinical and research interviews with individuals and families over the past 25 years. Life histories were constructed from longitudinal interviews—that is, sequences of regularly scheduled 1-hr interviews that extended over periods of time ranging from several weeks to a few years. The frequency of these meetings averaged about one interview every 2 weeks (Hall, 1990b).

Observations and specific probe questions were also used in collection of data. The author's individual, family, and organizational practices in clinical sociology were primary settings for this documentation (Hall, 1990a, 1991). Although the clinical interviews necessarily dealt primarily with clients' varied presenting problems, many value choices discussed related both directly and indirectly to identity and religion (Berger & Luckmann, 1967).

In addition to clinical interviews, the author conducted approximately 100 research interviews. These interviews focused solely on delineating influences of religious and spiritual beliefs in defining identity (Hall, 1986b, 1991). The interpersonal and structural research data collected in these interviews suggest correlations between individual and group identities and religions or beliefs (Mol, 1978). Community interventions through discussion groups, workshops, and retreats yielded further life history data, as well as increased opportunities to apply identity empowerment theory to issues of identity and religion and to develop viable clinical and intervention techniques.

Thus, this book derives from summations and distillations of life history data and facts related to interactive processes and social structures. The issue of whether individual contributions can have a lasting impact on social institutions and society is examined. The life history, organizational, community, and societal data suggest patterns and themes that show how individual and group identities are strengthened by making specific value choices, and how identities make a difference in patterns of social interaction and qualities of social life.

The data were also used to outline interdependencies among beliefs, values, social structures, and individual and group identities (Hall, 1991). Particular attention was given to data that suggest patterns of behavior associated with individual responsibilities, families, gender, social classes, cultures, and society, and thus clarify the already established "everydayness" of religious beliefs and practices (Berger & Luckmann, 1967; Lenski, 1961).

THEORETICAL SOURCES

This book has multiple theoretical sources. Religions themselves, in fact, can also be thought of as early or rudimentary forms of theorizing about the nature of the universe and the nature of human nature (Durkheim, 1915). For example, early Hinduism contained statements about the nature of individual and social being over long periods of time. In later historic periods, moral philosophy—a more secular, academic endeavor—was also much preoccupied with understanding the complexities surrounding these issues (Cooley, 1964; Mead, 1934).

Sociological theories (Macionis & Benokraitis, 1995) and Dr. Murray Bowen's (1978) pioneering work in family systems theory are more recent theoretical sources of this book. The 10 concepts of identity empowerment theory—self, dyad, triad, family, religion, definition of the situation, reference group, class, culture, and society—form a frame of reference that links patterns of behavior and small group interaction with broad social processes and structures, as well as combines subjective and objective perspectives. (See the appendix to this book for a more detailed description of identity empowerment theory.)

Identity empowerment theory is a synthesis of structural-functional theory; conflict theory; and cultural theory, which includes symbolic interaction theories and interpretive sociology (Hall, 1990a). These three major theoretical paradigms emphasize the significance of social structures and functions, resources, and values, respectively, in determining individual and social behavior. Because identity empowerment theory is largely based on the premise that value choices can bring about substantial personal and social changes, deliberate selections of goals and ideals as effective strategies for modifying interpersonal relationships and social structures, as well as for improving individual and group functioning, are emphasized in this book (Hall, 1991).

From societal and sociological viewpoints, this book is based more on Weber's theory of meaningful social action than on Marx's materialism (Macionis & Benokraitis, 1995). More attention is given to ideals than to economic assets. Values and symbols—which are central components of symbolic interaction theories, interpretive sociology, and cultural theory—are also examined in the analyses of decision making and behavior related to identity and beliefs (Cooley, 1964; McNamara, 1992; Mead, 1934).

METHODOLOGY

To collect sufficient life history data from more than 1,000 individuals and families, the author conducted regularly scheduled weekly, biweekly, or monthly longitudinal interviews over periods of time ranging from a few weeks to several years. Many of the questions asked in these interviews were open-ended, including follow-up probe queries to yield more intimate details of family and interpersonal functioning. Each interview lasted approximately 1 hr, and the author was the only person to conduct the series of individual and family interviews.

The author constructed ethnographies of several organizations and documented specific social and community interventions. Different kinds of discussion groups provided additional sources of life history data, as well as opportunities to observe varied patterns of interaction. In all cases, individual and social interventions were planned and observed, and their impacts on individuals, organizations, and communities were assessed.

Experiential data were also gathered through participant observation, in which the author essentially became a member of ongoing exchanges in families and other kinds of social and community discussion groups. In addition, everyday, informal settings were used to determine patterns of interaction within and among social classes, and to make broad institutional analyses. The social data were combined with the life history data from clinical and research interviews to more fully document the scope and complexity of issues related to identity and religion or belief systems.

Secondary analyses of relevant research findings were used to conceptualize additional critical aspects of interdependencies between identity and religion. Where patterns in data were sufficiently consistent, these data were used as sources for formulating the 10 basic concepts of identity empowerment theory. These concepts not only formed a theoretical base for examining identity and religion, but also guided further collection of data. In this way, theories and methods became essentially interchangeable in the author's quest to make effective clinical interventions through defining identity in relation to religion and other belief systems.

IDENTITY EMPOWERMENT THEORY

Identity empowerment theory explains some of the complex substantive connections between self and society. Its 10 basic concepts assess human dependencies and relationships to social institutions. Propositions based on identity empowerment theory suggest clinical strategies to improve the functioning of individuals and groups whereby clients make clearer and more decisive value commitments for themselves.

Identity empowerment theory is based on the premise that personal and social identities both derive from social sources and have social consequences. Religions can be thought of as critically important composites of values and ideals, which may become goals and objectives for individuals or groups who are working toward being effective moral agents in the complex interplay of society and history (Hall, 1991).

Family emotional interdependencies frequently limit individual functioning (Bowen, 1978); similarly, any emotional system may inhibit individual and group functioning. However, value choices made in accordance with religions or belief systems can increase motivations to discover ways out of these restrictive social influences. Furthermore, values derived from religions or belief systems can provide the means to increase social mobility, as well as to reinforce individual and group status.

Identity empowerment theory is a broad base of interrelated concepts from which central ideas related to identity and religion or belief systems can be examined. Ultimately, identity and religion need to be thought of, and acted upon, within the contexts or perspectives of community, society, history, and evolution (Ashbrook, 1993). It is for this reason that identity empowerment theory is a meaningful frame of reference for such examinations of identity and religion. Identity may be best understood as a result of value choices about ultimate realities and definitions of the universe (Progoff, 1985). By contrast, secular world views, although important and significant in their own right, all too often prove to be unnecessarily limiting for the purpose of successfully and effectively empowering identities (Appleyard, 1993).

Identity empowerment is possible because both identity and human behavior are expressions of specific kinds of orderliness in the universe (Mead, 1934). These facts make identity empowerment theory a sufficiently predictable basis with regard to formulations of strategies for clinical interventions. Both individual and collective behavior are strongly influenced by values or qualities that have been automatically or decisively incorporated into identities (Mol, 1987). Therefore, to change behavior, changing the kinds of values selected and integrated into identities is essential (Hall, 1990a). In fact, making value choices is one of the most dependable means to increase individual and social mobility, and to make other individual and social changes (Martin, 1990). Furthermore, this strategy is frequently more effective in accomplishing change than only trying to change behavior (Hall, 1991).

CLINICAL INTERVENTIONS

Communities mediate influences and patterns of behavior that result from inter-actions between individuals and society (Clark, 1990). To understand the impact of historical changes on identity and religion, one must first conceptualize the impact of communities on individuals and society (Glassner & Freedman, 1979). Such perspectives on individuals and societies enable clinicians to make effective interpersonal changes. This broad approach provides more meaningful contexts for clinical interventions than the relatively restricted intrapsychic or behavioral frames of reference conventionally used by many clinicians (Bowen, 1978).

Adequate theoretical sources, life history and behavioral data, and reliable methodologies are all necessary components of successful clinical interventions. Furthermore, a scientific model of knowledge can increase accuracy, purpose, and direction in clinical efforts, including those that focus on identity and reli-gion (Bowen, 1978). Although random efforts to understand and change behav-ior may prove to be effective in the short run, when theories and methodologies are deliberately applied to understanding and changing complex constellations of behavior, more consistent and more lasting clinical results are predictably accomplished (Bowen, 1978).

Religion is at the core of many different kinds of communities, in that beliefs and values form the substance of social consensus and legitimation (Hechter et al., 1993); this is particularly true of preliterate societies and early biblical periods. To the extent that identities are considered in relation to religions and value choices, clients are more meaningfully connected or bonded with their values (Progoff, 1985). When sufficient numbers of individual changes have been implemented, community and societal changes inevitably result (Glassner & Freedman, 1979). Thus, individual and group identities can be catalysts for broad social changes. Furthermore, selecting those values that essentially make up religious and social ideals can serve to keep individuals and communities connected with broad social institutions and trends (Jung, 1933).

Clinical strategies that link religion and identity empower individuals as mem-bers of communities (Hall, 1991). Clinicians benefit from familiarizing them-selves with broad theoretical bases; knowing and applying these concepts en-ables them to play more significant and more effective professional roles in facilitating clients' individual changes (Glassner & Freedman, 1979).

RELIGION, SPIRITUALITY, AND EMPOWERMENT

By using their own specific terms, religions divide beliefs and behaviors into categories of good and evil, as well as categories of sacred and banal or profane

(Durkheim, 1915; Warner, 1993). For example, totemic beliefs frequently re-volve around these dichotomies. The power of religions or belief systems as motivating forces is evident at both individual and group levels of interaction, and both sacred and secular powers need to be assessed in understanding the influence of religion on behavior (Hess, 1991). For example, when people be-lieve that they are doing what is right in the eyes of their God, they can trans-cend many harsh daily realities (Schumaker, 1992).

Both religion and spirituality—that is, less formalized beliefs in supernatural powers that encourage contemplative action—are motivators for the attainment of goals that may at first appear impossible to achieve. (See Chapters 5 and 7 for more information.) Religion and spirituality are also powerful sources of inspiration, in that their universal, ultimate dimensions open up myriad possi-bilities for being and doing (Tillich, 1952). For example, new world views are derived from religious and spiritual beliefs, as well as new views of human nature (Strunk, 1979). Religions can put lives into perspectives that include acknowledgments of ultimate concerns, as well as other critical dimensions of more universal experiences (Hess, 1991). Religions and spirituality allow people and things to be seen in a new light, broaden thinking, and promote consider-ations of individual lives and actions from transcendental viewpoints (Schu-maker, 1992).

Unlike religion, spirituality emphasizes individual devotion and enlighten-ment, even though this awareness may also connect individuals to the uni-verse and to other human beings (James, 1969). Mystics and contemplatives are models for people who want to lead spiritual lives (Teilhard de Chardin, 1965), and spirituality may be thought of as the essence of enlightened everyday be-havior (Ashbrook, 1993; Hall, 1986b; Spretnak, 1982).

Sometimes the routes to becoming spiritual are secular (Tillich, 1952); for example, people may be shocked into reassessing their beliefs through the death of a loved one. However, maintaining spiritual awareness and using spiritual resources are necessarily linked to religions, ideals, and values (Berger & Luck-mann, 1967). At some level, even religious believers have to maintain spiritual or individualized beliefs if they are to participate meaningfully in religious com-munities (Appleyard, 1993; Hall, 1991; Hammond, 1992; McNamara, 1992).

However, whether individuals aim to be religious or spiritual, their identities can be empowered in these developmental processes (Randour, 1993). Both religions and spirituality change individuals' world views and thereby have direct consequences for behavior (Strunk, 1979). Religion and spirituality in-crease awareness of individual connectedness to the universe at large (Butter-worth, 1969; Teilhard de Chardin, 1965) and of the role that sacred beliefs play in identities (Mol, 1978).

The dominant concept in both religious and spiritual belief systems is that of supernatural powers (Ashbrook, 1993). Human beings may be thought of as being overwhelmed by these powers, as being equal to them, or as being in partnership with them (Chopp, 1989). Their actions consequently depend on their views of themselves in relation to supernatural powers (Haney, 1989). This book explores the nature of these associations between individuals and supernatural powers, and emphasizes consideration of the implications of these associations for effective clinical practices.

Chapter 2

Setting the Scene

Identity issues are serious and compelling, especially when they relate to religions and spiritual beliefs (Mol, 1978). For example, the issue of religious conversion hinges on concerns about religious identity. Persisting in discovering and creating identities through making value choices increases the ability to move in constructive directions throughout life (Hall, 1990a), and being guided by a "higher self" leads predictably to living more fully and more effectively (James, 1969). Another result is that constructive empirical consequences and dividends derive from merging religious and mental health concerns (Schumaker, 1992).

Religions are repositories of society's most sacred traditions and most cherished values, which bespeak a higher order than that suggested by the banal realities of everyday life (Jung, 1933). For example, Protestantism is dominant in the formation of cultural values in the United States. Aligning the self with some of these much-respected traditions and values increases motivation to express ideals through actions that make contributions to others and the common good (Weber, 1958).

Religions tie individuals to higher self, to beliefs in the sacred, to communities, and to society (Yinger, 1957). Through devotional practices, awareness of "oneness" with a supreme deity or supernatural realities, and with other people, is increased (Durkheim, 1915). In this way individuals may live more fully because they believe they serve as conduits of supernatural powers, desiring only to respond better to these otherworldly powers (Weber, 1958).

Beliefs—especially beliefs about the sacred—have strong influences on identities, whether their holders are aware of this relationship or not, and identities in large part define behavior (Luckmann, 1967). For example, if individuals believe that they are children of God, they behave differently than if they believe that they are products of sin or creatures with animal passions (Strunk, 1979). However, human beings are not determined solely by either outside or inside forces, and they can choose how they create their identities (Randour,

1993). In fact, a primary responsibility of humans is to make such choices and definitions wisely, so as to make real social contributions and gain life satisfaction (Wuthnow, 1991).

A first step toward understanding some of the complexities in the relationship between identity and religion is to examine one's thoughts and feelings about oneself (James, 1969). To further this understanding, it is important to observe one's interactions with others, particularly with relatives and those who are emotionally significant (Cooley, 1964). These observations help to assess the extent of independence and interdependence in actions, as well as the extent of reactivity to others' pressures and expectations. For example, individuals must be able to assess their own autonomy in relation to parental influences. Families are frequently sites of oppression for women; getting free from their exploitative pressures may result from uncovering some of the intricacies and nuances of these restrictive relationship systems (Collins, 1990).

Historically, families usually decide which religious communities their members join and the degree to which specific religious beliefs are accepted. For example, a father may choose to have his children attend Jewish religious school throughout childhood and adolescence. Thus people are born into religions rather than choose them of their own accord (Lenski, 1961). As a consequence, it is generally particular relatives who serve as the most direct and therefore the most influential role models for following particular beliefs and practices, rather than traditional religious leaders per se (Bowen, 1978).

Furthermore, established patterns in family dependencies and interaction are reflected in any given family's modes of worship (Johnson, 1973). To a large extent, families that have fewer ritualized patterns of interaction also have more flexible religious beliefs and practices (Fromm, 1967). In fact, a family's religious belief system is more directly determined by the degree and content of parents' and grandparents' religious commitments than by more impersonal contacts with religious institutions themselves (Bowen, 1978).

SELF

Self is the individualized source and reserve of individuals' deepest beliefs and commitments (Cooley, 1964; Mead, 1934), and individuals are moral agents who have some freedom to take charge of their lives (Teilhard de Chardin, 1965). Although human impulses are frequently nonrational, there are also distinct human capacities to direct behavior through making choices. For example, to some extent people can choose whether to be victims or to make efforts to overcome their social disadvantages. Because cherished personal and social values are the most significant elements of self, the content of these values is an important influence on behavior and interaction (Jung, 1933; Progoff, 1985; Tillich, 1952).

Acting from self as a moral agent implies that, compared to the range of possibilities for human creativity, the production and expression of self are more significant activities than other kinds of behavior (James, 1969). Views of the world, society, culture, social classes, religion, and families depend on self-conceptions and identities, and these make real differences in human behavior and clients' progress in psychotherapy (Strunk, 1979). Thus, self can be thought of as the core of thoughts and beliefs, and identity as symbolic links of the self to selected social values and meanings (Goffman, 1959).

Self is the most feasible starting point for defining some of the interactions between identity and religion (Hall, 1991). Self creates identity, and may use religion as a resource or tool to accomplish this task. However, whether or not a person refers to religion directly for developmental purposes, the self is a moral agency that makes life-defining decisions and distills uniqueness. Self is an emotional standpoint and center of reactivity, as well as a base for the cultivation of moral attitudes and the initiation of actions (Ashbrook, 1993).

Deliberately building the self and monitoring one's reactivity to others uncovers possibilities for establishing the ties between identity and religion. Vigilance clarifies observations of consequences of actions and discernment of preferred values. Awareness of the personal and social effects of choosing to honor one value or another through trial and error behavior enhances decisiveness about one's actions (Mead, 1934).

Self has boundaries, and the viability of these boundaries must be maintained. Although these boundaries should remain permeable to some extent—it is disadvantageous as well as impractical to cultivate overly rigid definitions of self—the core of self needs firmly held convictions and beliefs for protection against the push and pull of everyday circumstances and interactions (Smith, 1987).

A persistent danger in intimate two-person relationships is that boundaries of self are violated when one person moves into the other person's space. This process can be cozy, intense, and enjoyable in the short run, but it is destructive in the long run. Too much involvement with each other becomes threatening and frequently conflictual. A primary mutual concern must be to achieve or sustain autonomy if relationships are to endure. If this priority is not actively recognized, freedom to live fully is inevitably lost. In their capacities as sources of values, meanings, and ideals, religions are particularly useful for making choices to define the self clearly and maintain these boundaries (Randour, 1993).

SOCIAL STRUCTURES

Although the concept of social structure may suggest remoteness from daily experiences, everyone contributes to and is affected by structures such as social stratification systems and social institutions (Butterworth, 1969; Mead, 1934). For practitioners, the relatedness and impact of social structures need to be kept in mind while going about one's daily business and while working with clients in clinical settings. Furthermore, insofar as religion is a basic social institution, it is beneficial to know how specific religious structures affect identities and behavior (Schumaker, 1992).

Historically, five basic social institutions have been considered as sustaining society—family, religion, the economy, education, and the political system (Macionis & Benokraitis, 1995). These institutions reinforce each other and permeate social stratification systems (Hall, 1981). However, because social institutions are necessary for the survival of society rather than individuals, most related social structures limit rather than enhance individual freedom (Appleyard, 1993). In fact, it appears that perhaps only those structures that are deliberately organized to promote freedom can do so (Haney, 1989).

Social classes—status categories are based on economic resources, age, sex, race, ethnicity, or religion—provide evidence that there are more institutionalized limitations on people with few valued resources than among those who are relatively well endowed with resources (Macionis & Benokraitis, 1995). Thus, variations in opportunities are directly related to individual and group placements in social hierarchies (McGuire, 1994). However, upper-class members of society—those with substantial economic resources—may have extremely inhibiting religious beliefs and restrictive religious affiliations because of the rigidity of their ritualistic, traditional lifestyles (Hammond, 1992). Also, just as social stratification systems are major influences on the maintenance of conformity and status definitions throughout society, social classes themselves are characterized by specific subcultures (Mol, 1978). For the purpose of understanding the complex interplay of identity and religion, it is advantageous to consider that social classes have specific religious styles, which may include either denominational or sectarian religious forms (Goode, 1968). Generally speaking, denominations tend to be peopled by upper social classes, and sects by lower social classes (Herberg, 1955).

VALUE CHOICES

One of the ways in which people exert some control over their identities, particularly over the ideals they internalize, is through the kinds of value choices they make on a daily basis (Berger & Luckmann, 1967). For example, where and how one spends leisure time can express different beliefs and values. Religions and belief systems come alive or stay vital when conscious decisions are made about accepting or rejecting their specific values (McNamara, 1992). Scrutiny of values, deliberation about values, and interpretations of religious meanings all create identity.

Strengthening capacities and increasing opportunities to make everyday value choices enhance human dignity and ensure possibilities for creating purpose and direction (Berger & Luckmann, 1967). Value choices imply a hierarchy of preferences and ideals (Lenski, 1961). The social contexts of values in society also suggest a ranking of more or less acceptable or legitimate ideals, and the human dilemma can be described as that of making necessary choices from these options (McGuire, 1994). Unless values are carefully selected, unwanted values may control behavior and life outcomes (Goffman, 1959); that is, individuals may easily become victims of unchosen influences without knowing it (Randour, 1993).

Thus, value choices are the lifeblood of identities (Hall, 1990b). Taking firm stands in relation to others and making substantial contributions to society are only possible through grounding the self in constructive, life-enhancing values, which themselves necessarily derive from society (Progoff, 1985). Human beings act according to their convictions; and unless they choose the specific value sources of their convictions, their actions are ineffective and lack meaning (Haney, 1989).

FAMILIES

Families generally define individuals' first experiences of religion, or their experiences of not having religion. For example, the concept of God may be presented as having great importance at an early age or not mentioned at all. The characteristics of supernatural beings are initially learned from parents or relatives, who instruct members of younger generations how to pray and participate in religious services (Bowen, 1978). The religious style or culture of a family is communicated to all family members, especially to those who are dependent and therefore vulnerable (Spretnak, 1982).

Although it is neither necessary nor perhaps even advisable to try to duplicate the parents' religious beliefs in the child, many people do not in fact change their original religious affiliations (Malony & Southard, 1992). Parental indoctrinations may frequently persist as extremely powerful influences in adult religious experiences, whether or not those same beliefs are fully accepted (Hussain, 1984).

To the extent that any given family's religious beliefs are relatively closed—that is, they are not open to question or scrutiny—the emotional tone of religious and other experiences will predictably be dogmatic (Bowen, 1978). A high degree of dogma or bigotry creates many different kinds of family problems and crises (Bendroth, 1994). For example, when emotionally significant family members espouse dogmatic religious beliefs, there is more authoritarianism, less questioning, more rebellion, more conflict, and more cutting off from other family members in that family system. Thus, in many instances the intensity of family religious beliefs influences the identity and behavior of family members as much as, if not more than, the content of those beliefs (Fromm, 1967).

Families are the foundations of basic views of self, and several generations of family interaction reveal the strength and durability of particular patterns of dependency behavior (Bowen, 1978). In fact, individual freedom to pursue religion and specific religious values may be severely limited, or may not exist, unless these kinds of family pressures are dealt with effectively. Individuals may convert to new religions, but to some extent they have to continue to deal with parental bigotry. However, identities can be strengthened by seeing the continuing interactive influences of families and religions, and their impacts on autonomy (Johnson, 1973).

RELIGION

One of the most important properties of religions is that they provide many people with belief systems and frames of reference for viewing the self, the world, and the universe (Mol, 1978). Religions tie individuals to particular traditions and social structures through their beliefs and practices (Durkheim, 1951). However, because religions are social products—even though they are believed to be "divinely" inspired—they necessarily reflect society and human nature, and must respond to community needs to exist (Van Zandt, 1991).

Religions, because of their intrinsic symbolism, provide meanings, purpose, and direction (Stark & Glock, 1968). They can thus motivate individuals and groups to do things that might otherwise be experienced as boring or even distasteful. For example, Judaism places so much emphasis on education and tradition that studying the difficult language of Hebrew is undertaken fairly easily by very young Jewish children. Optimally, religions suggest vocations and innovations, as well as provide means to celebrate life, rather than merely encourage accommodation to unpleasant conditions (Yinger, 1957). In fact, both joyful rituals and mourning ceremonies are critical components of religious practices (Durkheim, 1915).

Because religions facilitate a transcendence of daily life, they offer solutions or ways out of difficult predicaments (Pargament, Kennell, Hathaway, Grevengoed, Newman, & Jones, 1988). Religions answer questions about the nature of ultimate reality, and, through mechanisms such as prayer and meditation, they offer invisible means of communication with supernatural powers (Luckmann, 1967). Because religions are dependent on families for recruiting new members, there are close correlations—frequently engendering conflicts of interests—between religious concerns and family issues. However, even though religions generally present themselves as sustaining family life, religious models of families are frequently traditional and conservative, and therefore relatively out of touch with contemporary changes and needs (Johnson, 1973).

Identities can be enriched by religion (Mol, 1978). For example, people who believe that they are children of God are more likely to be able to empower or re-create themselves. Even though human beings are necessarily limited by social institutions and classes, religions provide motivations to overcome or modify these same structures. Religions can inspire and galvanize individuals and groups into action, and religions can facilitate social mobility, a momentum that helps to neutralize the restrictive impact of social structures (Yinger, 1957).

SOCIAL CLASSES

Different social classes have varied religious styles. For example, during the urbanization of the industrial revolution in England, Methodist practices kept workers in their places and motivated them to work hard. In general, the higher the social class, the more denominational the religious affiliation (Yinger, 1957). Sectarian associations, on the other hand, are more characteristic of lower social classes and minority groups—that is, groups that are less powerful and more peripheral than mainstream groups (Beckford & Luckmann, 1989).

The degrees of association between social stratification and religion influence identity and the capacity to change identity (Mol, 1978). Furthermore, religions can increase motivation to modify social stratification systems themselves, rather than merely serve as sources of motivation for individuals to be socially mobile or to accept the status quo. For example, Protestantism boosts individual efforts to achieve and raise social status through accomplishments. However, unlike class cultures, religions ultimately have universal appeal. In fact, it is vital for religions to maintain this kind of broad perspective as a basis for thinking and action if people are to be able to effectively increase the social good (Appleyard, 1993).

Power issues are also reflected in religions and religious organizations (Cornwall, 1987). To the extent that social classes are distinguished from each other by differential access to power, their related religious organizations may similarly limit people's access to supernatural powers, or to the leaders of those religious organizations (Ryan, 1992). However, identification with the life of the universe through religious beliefs facilitates the transcendence of many worldly or secular concerns about power, as well as the achievement of self-definitions and objectives that go beyond social class lifestyles and status expectations (Stark & Glock, 1968).

Utopian models of heaven, or a perfect society, are frequently egalitarian rather than hierarchical (Manuel & Manuel, 1979). Similarly, the substance of many religious belief systems challenges existing social stratification (Smith, 1991). When the universalism of religions in modern industrial societies motivates individuals to claim their heritage as divine beings, it frequently runs counter to secular definitions of rights and responsibilities within social class systems (Roof, 1992).

CULTURES

Cultures are made up of secular beliefs and values, which are ultimately either merged with or juxtaposed to societal consensus (Hechter et al., 1993). In pluralistic societies many subcultures coexist, sometimes with their own intrinsic conflicts and contradictions, and sometimes in opposition to other subcultures and mainstream society (Wilson, 1986).

The norms and standards accepted by the majority of the population, or by the majority of members in the most powerful groups of society, make up the dominant culture. For example, middle-class standards dominate popular culture in the United States. Minority group cultures essentially compete with this mainstream culture, become integrated into it, or stand outside it, frequently in adversarial positions (Martin, 1990). However, people cannot avoid the influence of other cultures because historical values pervade society. Deliberate choices about which values to accept or reject must be made by individuals so as not to become mere by-products of a particular culture or subculture (Stark & Bainbridge, 1985).

To make sense out of the many complexities in cultural trends and patterns, religions can be viewed as an evolutionary source of modern secular cultures (Ashbrook, 1993). Cultures can also be thought of as either traditional or modern, individual- or community-oriented, and as consisting of either life-enhancing, constructive values or restrictive, destructive values.

In considering the complexities in relationships between identity and religion, individuals can be thought of as inhabitants of particular cultural climates. People participate in many different secular cultures, and each religion creates its own culture; these sources provide values for a particular society. Cultures are reservoirs of socially preferred values, which are nourished by attention and ultimately expressed in behavior (Stark & Glock, 1968).

SOCIETY

Identification with religions provides meaningful and empowering links between individuals and society (Hall, 1981, 1990a). Identities are tied to particular values, and religions give meanings and structures to those values with which people identify. Identity and religion are bridges between individuals and society, and society is a vital vantage point from which to review and understand the interactive influences of identity and religion. Seeing the self in this broad context makes a full assessment of goals and contributions possible, and sharpens the senses of direction and purpose.

Becoming a historical actor in society includes sufficient empowerment to initiate or participate in change processes. Gandhi, for example, was able to mobilize sufficient influence to precipitate Indian independence. All daily choices have significant individual and social consequences (Goffman, 1959; Smith, 1987), and opportunities to make changes flow from basic dignities and freedoms of human and religious heritages. Responsibility requires living up to potentials, rather than accepting narrow secular definitions of roles and stereotypes (Eisler, 1987).

Thinking of the self as an isolated individual, without awareness of identification with society, results in cutting the self off from others and inevitably suffering from self-estrangement (Clark, 1990). Religions help to bring individuals back into communities; they symbolize bonds with the human race, as well as characteristics of shared divine heritages. Religions are time-tested means of survival and fulfillment, which consistently give meaning to what otherwise might be meaningless experiences (Haught, 1984).

At best, religions empower identity so that continuous motivation to make constructive contributions to society is possible. Not habitually considering social contexts means that specific responsibilities remain unclaimed and unclear. However, in reality no one escapes influencing others, and each person necessarily has some impact on social structures and processes. Human beings do not live in vacuums, but rather in rich milieus. Even though individuals may not make original, creative contributions to the whole, especially if they are relatively inactive and passive, in the final analysis they inevitably support the status quo status quo (Gerth & Mills, 1953). Responsibilities consist largely of knowing and deciding where to invest human energies (Hammond, 1992).

QUESTIONS AND ANSWERS

Perhaps the most important question to ask at the outset of this examination of identity and religion is "To what extent do social influences determine behavior?" Although this is a question that cannot be answered with precision, personal experiences and observations suggest that people are socialized beings, and that qualities of life are strongly influenced by status in basic social institutions and social classes.

A significant follow-up question is "Do social institutions or social classes have a stronger influence over behavior?" The most reliable answer to this is that all five basic social institutions—family, religion, the economy, education, and the political system—influence patterns of interaction, as well as social class memberships, cultures, and society at large. This broad-based answer suggests that individuals are little more than points of possible action in complex social systems, and that patterns of interdependencies within and between these systems strongly influence behavior.

To the extent that it is believed that emotional aspects of being have the strongest sway over decisions and behavior, this question will be answered differently. Scrutinizing experiences may lead to a conclusion that family dependencies and religious beliefs are more compelling determinants of thinking and behavior than other social institutions or social classes. Thus families and religions may influence behavior more strongly than other social institutions or social classes.

A further basic question for orienting understanding of identity and religion is "What assumptions are made about the nature of human nature?" In focusing on discovering how to change behavior, models of human nature must include sufficient openness for those changes. Even though conditions that promote change may be more hypothetical than real, it is necessary to believe that some margin of flexibility for change and adaptation exists if identity and religion are to be fully understood.

GENERALIZATIONS

To specify some of the major influences related to identity and religion, explanations must be built from meaningful and representative generalizations. First, even though diverse religions have distinctively rich and varied characteristics, some of the common denominators among religions may have the strongest impact on identities. For example, religions provide clusters of values that create perspectives for viewing the self and others in relation to each other and the world. Another shared characteristic of religions is that they are social and moral sources that serve as guides for decision making.

To deepen the understanding of identity and religion, a context that gives a full picture of their relationships and interdependencies must be formulated. Identity cannot be understood only by examining religion, but must also be studied by scrutinizing patterns of interaction in families, the economy, education, the political system, and social classes. Actions must be considered in their appropriate contexts.

One consequence of individuals' serious consideration of the complex linkages between identity and religion is the individuals' realization of some of the advantages of allowing a higher self to guide behavior. Furthermore, this process will allow individuals to determine whether they do really experience increased advantages in following this higher self.

Another key generalization about identity and religion is that a significant goal for people who want to be empowered is to be autonomous. Whatever values and dictates characterize a religion, making individual interpretations and decisions is more influential in strengthening identity than conforming to particular religious traditions or rituals.

PROPOSITIONS

Assuming that there are regularities in the universe, and that facts and observations about identity and religion can be correlated, several propositions can be formulated. These propositions address relationships between and among variables, or individual and social influences, and postulate that specific patterns or trends repeat and have recognizable consequences.

One proposition about identity and religion is that this alignment between self and cherished values brings with it predictable behavioral consequences. The stronger a person's identity, through deliberately made value choices, the more constructive the interpersonal and social behavior that flows from this alignment. The more this identity is refined through making deliberate value choices, the more individual and social behavior is constructive.

Another proposition related to identity and religion is that behavior is governed by relationships between social institutions and social classes, and that these social structures themselves are products of social interaction. Shifts in the balance among these structures bring about individual and social changes, and, to make sure that constructive changes occur, alignments between identity and religions must be examined.

CHOICES

It is useful to outline some choices that will improve the quality of life. For example, an individual who chooses education rather than violence clearly moves in a direction of life enhancement. Other options for progression rather than regression can be clarified, as well as individual and social consequences of choosing one value over another. Deciding which values are cherished most precipitates motivations and ways to honor those values.

Choices may be difficult for individuals to define, but it is essential to move in one direction or another, and this realization impels decisions. If options about values and directions are not chosen, others may take control of these possibilities. A predisposition to succumb to social pressures limits an individual's freedom to respond satisfactorily to others' expectations.

Choices are omnipresent and omnipotent, and people cannot escape responsibilities to make choices, however hard they may try. Lines of least resistance emerge and take over a life unless decisions are clear. For example, in crises individuals may act automatically rather than thoughtfully. Thus, a major challenge is to take charge of thoughts, feelings, and behavior. The following case exemplifies this argument.

CASE STUDY

Marcia Reynolds was a lower-class, 35-year-old African American woman brought up in a Southern Baptist religious and social community in a small town in South Carolina. As a child, Marcia had experienced many advantages from being raised in a closely knit extended family, whose members in large part attended church and church functions fairly regularly. Family members' ideas of respectability, responsibility, and social expectations were defined by these religious and social experiences, and Marcia was raised to have a clear sense of what was considered to be right and wrong, as well as what others expected of her.

However, before Marcia was 25 years old, she rebelled from her strict moral upbringing and gave birth to a son and a daughter without being married. Although the man who had fathered both her children still visited them fairly regularly, Marcia had to struggle to earn sufficient income to take care of them, because he could not assume these financial responsibilities. Marcia sought counseling to help her to establish priorities in the confusing and stressful situation of having to assume essentially full financial and moral responsibility for raising her son and daughter.

Specific conditions precipitated Marcia's crisis in parenting. Her mother had died within the past 6 months, from a lingering and painful case of cancer, and after this loss some of her closest relatives moved out of town. Marcia found it more difficult than ever to meet her child care responsibilities, because these relatives had formerly been willing to look after her children. Following her mother's death and her relatives' moves out of town, Marcia also suffered from recurring loneliness and depression.

Analysis

Within a few months of clinical work Marcia was able to assume new directions in her life. She persisted in pursing the immediate goals of completing her education and finding work, and she enrolled in classes to finish her high school equivalency certificate. These efforts were successful because Marcia valued education, and she was also able to see how completing her high school studies would be best for her children as well as for herself in the long run. Accomplishing this objective would also provide her with further opportunities for advanced study at a later date.

Marcia also decided to return to the religious community of her childhood and to resume participation in some of the church activities she had enjoyed as a youngster. Even though she had become somewhat out of touch with these connections, especially since her mother's recent illness and death, clear memories of earlier satisfactions remained and lured her back. As therapy broadened Marcia's emotional and intellectual horizons, she was able to satisfy some of her social needs in these ways.

Through discussions in clinical sessions, Marcia reactivated some of her former interests and skills in using prayer and meditation as support mechanisms. She found role models to emulate, particularly among older women in the church community, and the congregation gave her emotional support as well as some much-needed child care services. After a year of therapy, Marcia accepted a bookkeeping job in a small corporation, which promised to pay for college studies in accounting.

STRATEGIES FOR CLINICAL INTERVENTIONS

Most clinical exchanges take place in interpersonal contexts, although organizational and community interventions are also integral components of sociological practice. Clinical sociology conceptualizes the significance of human relatedness for individual and social health and well-being, whether this relatedness is at personal, organizational, community, or societal levels of analysis (Clark, 1990).

Because different kinds of clinical exchanges generally follow question and answer formats, creating specific discussion strategies is essential for accomplishing effective clinical interventions. Ideally, clinicians should formulate questions that heighten clients' awareness of who they are and what they want to do, and clinicians should encourage clients to express their own views rather than follow specific guidance. In no way should clinicians suggest or impose their values and standards on clients. Clients' values are precious resources for effective clinical interventions, and honoring applications of clients' values should be clinicians' highest priority. For example, clinicians should not recommend that clients study or acquire specific skills unless clients want to pursue such activities to meet their own needs and purposes. Only clients themselves know which goals they can be really motivated to accomplish.

Clinical strategies need to include thoughtful considerations of influences in society at large, as well as of interdependencies in domestic milieus. Progress in clinical interventions is essentially an expansive process that flows from clients' most cherished values, whether or not clients are aware of these connections. Therefore, unearthing clients' deepest values is a continuing goal in many different kinds of clinical exchanges. However, this process may be difficult, and may take a relatively long time, because values are directly related to personal growth, social commitments, and broad societal contexts. In other words, defining values amidst everyday behavior is inordinately complex, especially because clinicians may not have adequate knowledge of clients' everyday realities.

Whatever the academic disciplines and specific professional training of clinicians, it is essential for them to be able to put clients' lives in realistic perspective by examining the social contexts of their behavior. Placing clients in meaningful social contexts is largely an interdisciplinary enterprise. When clinicians help clients build broad pictures of their lives, clients get clearer senses of meaning and can estimate the individual and social consequences of their own value choices more accurately. Therefore, in considering the interactive influences of identity and religion, clinicians must pay attention to families, gender, the economy, education, and the political system, because identity and religion are inextricably related to these multiple aspects of social institutions and social stratification (Lenski, 1961). Identity and religion are embedded in society as well as in the deepest roots of each individual.

10 Clinical Tasks

1. Take extensive family histories of clients, and include facts and events in the lives of at least three generations of family members.
2. Using these life history data, highlight the most significant turning points in clients' lives.
3. Assess the extent to which clients value autonomy and freedom in their day-to-day activities.
4. List the strongest convictions and value commitments clients hold.
5. Ask clients to describe the broad picture of their lives.
6. Find out how clients see themselves.
7. Encourage clients to formulate one or two goals they want to accomplish.
8. Analyze what holds clients back from accomplishing their chosen goals.
9. Assess clients' positions in relation to the institutions and social structures of family, religion, class, culture, and society.
10. Support clients' attempts to move in their chosen directions.

Chapter 3

The Individual and Religion

Although religions frequently support the status quo, as Protestantism supports the ideology of individualism in the United States, they may at the same time paradoxically suggest directions for change and even promote innovation, as Protestantism expedited the industrial revolution (Ashbrook, 1993; Weber, 1958). Deities, supreme powers, and godheads to some extent symbolize societies; worshippers essentially revere specific aspects of societies or social changes in their worship rituals (Durkheim, 1915; Yinger, 1957).

Where religions are used and abused by those in power for the purpose of manipulating their subordinates, they inevitably serve as tools of oppression rather than as means of liberation (Fromm, 1967; Lenski, 1961). However, many connections that individuals make with society through their religious beliefs and practices can be freeing, especially when people understand that their own fulfillment is closely related to societal well-being (Wuthnow, 1991). In fact, some clinical data have substantiated direct correlations between divine relations, social relations, and individual and social well-being (Pollner, 1989).

One of the relatively negative and more restrictive pressures that religions impose on individuals is an imperative to conform to established beliefs and practices, as well as to conventional standards of behavior (Herberg, 1955). Case studies of religions give useful examples of individual and social consequences of being brainwashed rather than having opportunities to exercise choices (Barker, 1984; Bendroth, 1994). Even when religions advocate salvation, they frequently suggest and expect believers to follow specific prescribed routes to gain or reach that blessed state rather than advocate the exercise of individual initiative (Luckmann, 1967). Beliefs in religious cosmologies and practices are endorsed by implementations of negative and positive sanctions, which guide members in their everyday behavior but also restrict inventiveness (Hess, 1991).

Although many people choose not to be religious believers, religions necessarily affect everyone's life either directly or indirectly (Berger & Luckmann,

1967). Historical research on charismatic religious leaders, such as Saint Paul, documents how prophetic religious beliefs create many different kinds of secular consequences, thus highlighting the inevitability of religious and secular relatedness (Blasi, 1991). Therefore, even if religion is not salient to an individual's beliefs and values, religions have to be reckoned with in varied contexts, such as social classes, gender relations, families, the economy, education, and the political systems (Hammond, 1992).

SELF

Self can be thought of as the center or core of individual being. Self is synonymous with moral agency, and as such is the decision maker and mover of individuals' actions. To the extent that religions permeate intellectual and emotional milieus with specific values and beliefs, self must find ways to respond to this pervasiveness. Self selects values with which to identify and cherishes meaningful ideals. For example, a woman may decide to become a feminist and thereby change her priorities and goals. Thus, chosen values and ideals form the core of self and become sources of moral decisions and behavior.

Self is strengthened through the processes of selection and identification, and motivations to accomplish desired objectives are increased. Because religious sources of values are intrinsically social, human motivation cannot be fully understood without putting individual actions into contexts of religions and society (Hechter et al., 1993; McGuire, 1994). Thus religious experiences and social meanings overlap (Durkheim, 1915; James, 1969).

Self cannot be fully developed unless it is meaningfully connected to society (Cooley, 1964; Mead, 1934). In fact, unless individuals activate their connectedness to others, they may not be able to survive (Durkheim, 1951). Religions serve a very significant social purpose by linking selves to society through their belief systems of meanings and ritualistic community practices (Yinger, 1957). Furthermore, when people are alienated from their communities and social institutions, they may be reintegrated by participating in communities with shared religious beliefs and rituals (Pollner, 1989).

Optimally, the self must maintain individuality and autonomy throughout all kinds of religious participation, because it is freedom and the uniqueness of self that guide innovation and creativity (Hammond, 1992). High achievements in moral behavior are generally not synonymous with adaptations to society, but rather with working toward innovative socially valued goals that also further the well-being of all (Beckford & Luckmann, 1989).

IDENTITY

Identity functions as a bridge between self and society (Hall, 1990a). Identity consolidates the strongest and deepest meanings of values that the self selects from religion or secular sources, and generates impulses to action (Mol, 1978). Thus, selecting and expressing cherished values actively creates identities, and identities precipitate patterns of behavior that are congruent with these values (Stark & Glock, 1968). Research on conversion processes further highlights the links between identity and behavior in specific identity transitions and transformations, and suggests that stabilizing identity has some predictable behavioral consequences (Rambo, 1993).

Each person has continuing opportunities to build identity through value choices (Tillich, 1952). Because human socialization necessarily involves finding meanings, individuals must internalize either others' values or their own. Identities are consciously or unconsciously developed through encountering values, and identities are necessarily expressed through everyday actions (Smith, 1987).

Whereas deliberately internalizing life-enhancing values increases autonomy, accepting values accommodating to others predictably inhibits growth and expansiveness by compelling behavior that meets others' demands and expectations rather than one's own. For example, being creative as an artist requires much more skill than following other artists' styles of painting. To function optimally, individuals have to become connoisseurs of values and their behavioral consequences; making value choices is a responsibility that cannot be evaded, and there may be severe penalties for anyone who tries to do so. Thus identities are either created by self or are products of social institutions, such as the economy, which have impersonal needs to survive through societal adaptations.

It is personally and professionally useful to examine how identities relate to supernatural powers or a supreme reality. Examining the nature of human nature, and the range of possibilities for human bonds with the divine, helps to increase options and effectiveness in actions. Knowledge about influences of religions on behavior is further increased by observing and assessing everyday experiences of identifications. For example, it may be difficult for a Roman Catholic woman to deal with family planning and parenting issues.

Religions can be important baselines for strengthening identities, although some religious orientations, such as fundamentalism, may severely limit individual freedom (Marty & Appleby, 1991). Because religions provide an array of broad views and visions of the cosmos, identities become correspondingly expansive in scope when these kinds of values are internalized (Hall, 1986b).

Even secular values, such as those that make up contemporary sciences, may have powerful effects on individual souls in modern societies (Appleyard, 1993); and even technological inventions such as the birth control pill have transformed the quality of family life in the United States.

INDIVIDUAL

Developing the self and defining identity increase autonomy. Experiences show that strengthening uniqueness is an important and meaningful goal, and some religions suggest that it is only through individuals' being their true selves—or higher selves—that promises of divine heritage are fulfilled. However, to be as strong as possible, individuals must avoid geographical and emotional isolation, because interaction with significant others is necessary for the successful development of uniqueness, which can also sometimes be accomplished through exchanges in religious communities (Randour, 1993).

Developing individuality increases the likelihood of making constructive contributions to others. In some religions, such as Protestantism and Taoism, individuality can be thought of as a great treasure. These religious beliefs encourage valuing, cherishing, and expressing uniqueness, rather than conforming to particular traditional duties.

Individuality can be contrasted with togetherness. Although individuals may intend to do only that which they truly believe, others' pressures and expectations all too easily prompt them to conform to external influences. In fact, it frequently takes a great deal of effort to maintain individuality; it is much easier to give in to lines of least resistance and acquiesce to norms or well-established patterns of social behavior than to express uniqueness consistently (Bowen, 1978). Concentrating on expressing self and identity through practicing prayer and meditation is an effective means to increase the probability of becoming and remaining a real, authentic individual (James, 1969). Thus, optimal destinies can be seized by using religion as a prism through which to assess which values to select and cherish as inspiration and ideals (Progoff, 1985).

BELIEFS

Beliefs are philosophies or propositions about reality, which are usually held with varying degrees of emotional intensity (Berger & Luckmann, 1967). For some people, for example, a belief in the second coming of Christ may transform assessments of current social realities. Sometimes beliefs distort the realities of actual circumstances, or the human condition, and sometimes they are rational, empirically based, and in accordance with well-established properties of human nature and the universe (Schumaker, 1992). However, whatever the premises, formulating beliefs about reality has significant behavioral consequences. Buddhist beliefs about the significance of moral development, for example, contrast markedly with Calvinistic beliefs about the importance of achieving material success. Ideally, perceptions of facts, experiences, and others' knowledge and wisdom are congruent with personally forged truths, which frequently result from pain, crises, and life course turning points (Hall, 1986a).

Beliefs are sources of both heroic acts and demonic or bestial behavior. Great scientific or spectacular artistic achievements, as well as horrendous atrocities, can be expressions of particular belief systems. For example, the actions of Einstein and Hitler were products of belief systems, although these belief systems were markedly qualitatively different. Thus a vital human dilemma is to decide which beliefs to harbor and nurture.

Religious beliefs are distinguished from secular beliefs by their capacity to transcend many aspects of reality in relating to supernatural being. Although historically many religious beliefs have distorted knowledge or empirical truths, religious beliefs may play crucial constructive roles in facilitating human beings' effective adaptations to unknown situations, as well as effective coping with their deep fears and most fundamental concerns (Pargament et al., 1988).

Because religious beliefs play a major role in defining human nature, as well as human identities, they exert particularly critical influences on individual and social behavior (Lenski, 1961). In both visible and invisible ways, religions enter into everyday definitions of reality and relationships (Berger & Luckmann, 1967; Luckmann, 1967). Because human beings generally act from bases of beliefs, especially from bases of who they believe they are, efforts to accomplish difficult tasks cannot be sustained without some degree of vision and hope that go beyond any immediate problematic situations (Ashbrook, 1993; Progoff, 1985; Strunk, 1979).

VALUES

Values may be defined as an individual's or a group's most desired objectives or preferred goals (Eisler, 1987). Examples of widely shared values are freedom, justice, knowledge, truth, and enlightenment. Many values are agreed upon and deeply entrenched in cultures (Hussain, 1984). For example, traditional secular values like liberty and freedom have been supported by broad consensus through time (Kosmin & Lachman, 1993). Values are not idiosyncratic standards or aims, but rather socially cherished responses to historically shared concerns (Hechter et al., 1993).

Values may have vital life-enhancing properties like orienting individuals and groups for changes that enhance social well-being (Haney, 1989). They are consistently characterized by an objective reality, which does not become an individualized source of motivation until each person absorbs or internalizes specific meanings and related ideals (Berger & Luckmann, 1967). Because socialization consists of precisely these kinds of internalizations of values, the processes that culminate in absorptions of values become largely automatic (Mead, 1934). Therefore, unless some degree of awareness of value choices is cultivated, values that may more closely represent others' agendas than personally preferred objectives or desired ends can be internalized (Randour, 1993).

Values are the substantive cores of identities, and therefore the most vital focus for in-depth studies of identity and religion (Mol, 1978). For example, lives can be built upon nurturing the value of truth and expressing this value in behavior. Everyday behavior is driven by values, and behavior can only be effectively changed in the long run by changing values (Wilson, 1986). Internalizing or substituting transcendental religious values, such as Christian love or Jewish learning, for narrow secular values, such as an athletic lifestyle, predictably increases vision, purpose, and direction in behavior (Ryan, 1992).

Individual responsibility can be fruitfully thought of as using as much freedom and dignity as possible in making necessary value choices (Hammond, 1992). Taking charge of creating identities and regarding religions as sources of values increase individuals' awareness of being historical actors who can achieve constructive changes in society (Gerth & Mills, 1953). In fact, to some extent individuals and religions intersect and interact whenever a person makes value choices in constructing identity (Stark & Bainbridge, 1985).

Thus, values are critical building blocks of both religion and identity (Martin, 1990). Specific choices of values serve as essential preconditions for everyday achievements such as love of learning, material success, professional accomplishment, and disciplined living. Patterns of behavior are predictable consequences of value choices, especially of those values that are identified with most strongly (Kosmin & Lachman, 1993).

RELIGION

From the point of view of evolution, religions are narratives and practices that represent some of human beings' earliest efforts to understand and adapt to the universe (Ashbrook, 1993). Before scientific and behavioral theories were accepted or even considered, answers to shared fears and anxieties were built into and sought for through religions. For example, animism helped members of preliterate societies to adapt to their environment. Also, in many societies before their industrial and technological revolutions, education consisted largely of studying religions, such as Roman Catholicism, rather than of acquiring secular skills and knowledge (Bendroth, 1994; Finke & Stark, 1992; Luckmann, 1967).

Because of the long evolutionary development of religions such as Hinduism and Judaism, and because religions such as Taoism frequently explain evolution itself, there is no escaping the ubiquity of religious influences (Beckford & Luckmann, 1989). Even for nonbelievers, or for those who prefer to mix and match their beliefs by drawing upon several religious traditions, religions have a social reality and wield power in a wide variety of situations (Appleyard, 1993). Although modernists may view religions as archaic means of explaining the universe, because religions have survived with long histories, they cannot be viewed as inessential components of culture (Kaufman, 1993). In spite of the many anachronisms and contradictions that exist within sophisticated religious belief systems, such as present-day Roman Catholicism, many important values remain embodied in religions as well as sustained by them (Stark & Bainbridge, 1985).

One of the functional properties of religions is that they relate to the deepest parts of human concerns and feelings (Bendroth, 1994). Religions, including some of the earliest totemic belief systems, also provide codes and prescriptions on how to avoid evil and do good (Durkheim, 1915), and in this capacity religions suggest productive directions for developing a higher self (Randour, 1993). In fact, much of the importance of religions lies in their abilities to address broad social concerns as well as the most minuscule interpersonal needs (Schumaker, 1992). For example, Protestant world views have oriented economic enterprise as well as family life.

THE INDIVIDUAL AND RELIGION

To understand more about identity and religion, some of the most important dilemmas individuals face as they decide whether to be religious must be considered. For example, which religions or religious beliefs will advance individual growth and development must be assessed when deciding whether to become a practicing orthodox Jew. Religions to be avoided because of their capacities to inhibit or restrict individual strength, such as perhaps Confucianism, must also be determined thoughtfully rather than reactively.

In examining religions critically, attention must be paid to how supernatural powers and human nature are conceptualized, to assess whether specific beliefs imply that human beings are divine, whole, or flawed. Religious beliefs also postulate distance or closeness between human beings and supreme powers, relative access to supreme powers, and whether it is possible for people to have direct communications with supreme powers. If access to deities is a prerogative of religious leaders only, the nature of divine love must be defined, as well as what it means to love other people, and which moral codes apply to everyday life (Herberg, 1955).

The rigidity or flexibility of religious beliefs must also be scrutinized. For example, the dogmatic doctrines of Pentecostal sects can be more inhibiting than many Presbyterian practices. In some religions, negative sanctions are applied when some of the rules are not kept, and these penalties frequently sustain religious beliefs. Furthermore, modern secular knowledge may not easily fit into the world as envisioned by a specific religion, nor may it be easy or rewarding to be an autonomous self within a particular belief system.

Although religions may be accepted and practiced for their own sake, or for the purpose of perpetuating specific traditions, it is usually more beneficial to be objective and critical about selecting particular religious values to internalize than merely to absorb entire value systems obediently. Optimally, an individual's posture toward religion is that of critical but mature questioning of traditions and, at the same time, openness to new ideas.

Just as total acceptance of religions may not be wise, outright rejection of religion is perhaps equally foolhardy (Ellison, 1991). Ideally, people should know what they are looking for in personal and public values before they try to locate them in a particular religion. Even though it may be impossible to find exactly what they want within a given religion, it is better for individuals to have something in mind rather than nothing when trying to establish a firm sense of identity through exercising value choices (Gerth & Mills, 1953).

QUESTIONS AND ANSWERS

A basic question to ask in examining linkages between identity and religion is "To what extent do religions define identities?" If particular religions are salient, they define identities and selves more closely than if religions are not valued. However, even though religions may provide many basic beliefs, it is essentially individual interpretations of religious beliefs and practices that become more compelling and more vital determinants of attitudes and behavior. Identities are strengthened most when uniqueness is actively expressed through religions, rather than through mere obedience to religious precepts. Reasons for connections between identities and religions are uncovered by examining how supernatural powers symbolize societies. A belief in the omnipresent, omnipotent omniscience of God, for example, may be no more or no less than a symbolization of the universe in general, and society in particular. Religious belief systems are constructed largely to give lives meaning in the context of the great unknown.

Another question that gives a useful perspective on issues about individuality and religion is "What are the uses and abuses of religion?" Those who wield power in society frequently control the behavior of the masses by manipulating people's beliefs about current realities and the world to come, either after death or after a period of many years. These kinds of manipulations frequently subordinate and exploit relatively powerless members of society, so that present harsh realities are obfuscated or denied because attention is directed to a perfect life in the hereafter. Asking the question "Do religious beliefs distort or enhance reality?" facilitates reduction in the manipulations of religious beliefs and their negative consequences. When facts and myths are distinguished from each other, more constructive uses of religious beliefs can be made.

GENERALIZATIONS

The ability of religions either to support or to challenge society's status quo means that, at least hypothetically, both individuals and groups can decide to what extent they use religious sources to promote or inhibit change. One way to make the most constructive changes in society is deliberately to align yearnings for individual fulfillment with visions—often religious visions—of societal well-being. Realizing that more fulfillment comes about by participating in constructive social changes rather than in destructive processes, and acting accordingly, automatically deepens senses of meaning and increases behavioral effectiveness.

A useful way to understand the self, as well as links between identity and religion, is to think of the self as synonymous with moral agency. Personal integrity and convictions about what is right are closely tied to ideas about a higher self. Human beings are spiritual or moral as well as physical and mental, and they need to honor these basic characteristics in their behavior both to survive and to be fulfilled.

It is more important to select some religious values as sources of motivation than to accept wholeheartedly specific religious traditions. Being truly unique, as well as thoughtful and discriminating in selecting values for the cores of identities, makes the transcendence of harsh daily realities possible. The positive and negative sanctions of religions have limited usefulness in defining basic meanings when people want to develop as much of their potential as possible (Daly, 1968).

PROPOSITIONS

The more people honor traditional religious values, the less likely they are to be effective agents of change. By contrast, the more individuals honor values that emphasize innovative or creative ways of doing things, the more likely they are to be effective agents of change.

People necessarily have to make choices and assessments when deciding which values meet their needs for meaning. Having a clear vision of where to go, or how society should be, increases opportunities to move in the right direction. Clarity of vision can be achieved by coming to terms with the real meanings and empirical consequences of particular religious beliefs.

Viewing the self as a moral agent emphasizes the importance of making value choices to develop the higher self, and nurturing the higher self increases the likelihood of accomplishing constructive social changes. These linkages in behavior result from the interdependence of individual and social well-being. By definition, being a higher self includes caring deeply for the well-being of others, especially for those who are relatively disadvantaged.

The higher self is enhanced to the extent that uniqueness is developed, and spirituality depends on how much individuality is valued. Paradoxically, however, uniqueness is also linked to broad social needs and structural realities in society. Honoring the self requires addressing others' long term needs, and, although others' social expectations may not be met, moral rewards are gained by working toward accomplishing the greatest social good (Haney, 1989).

CHOICES

Deliberately choosing to move in a direction of developing a higher self at least makes the higher self a possibility. This basic choice is necessarily followed by many related choices, and developing the higher self must be a persistent goal and direction throughout daily life if it is to be accomplished.

Rather than following the established routes to salvation prescribed by dictates of traditional religious beliefs, it is frequently more viable to map out individual spiritual journeys. Only by being true to the self and to one's own cherished values can the higher self and social well-being be achieved.

Prayer and meditation are meaningful ways to express self and identity (Stark & Glock, 1968). These very personal activities join individuals to religions or religious beliefs, and heighten their awareness about universality and human interdependence. Thus, choosing to pray and meditate can strengthen one's identity and improve functioning in society.

The processes of selecting constructive beliefs automatically replaces negative beliefs, thereby purging behavior of distorted negative stereotypes and their destructive consequences. Identifying with creative values and beliefs enhances one's vision of society and makes choices to transcend reality more viable. Furthermore, discovering how to focus on optimal outcomes, rather than on existing harsh realities, increases awareness for making additional constructive choices (Randour, 1993).

In the following case study, the ability to think independently and make choices led to successful therapy.

CASE STUDY

Andrew Brown, a lower-class Protestant in his mid-30s, lived in a suburb in the northeastern part of the United States. Andrew was raised in a small family that espoused very formal Episcopalian beliefs and practices, which he found both stultifying and suffocating. In his early adulthood, Andrew suffered from serious depressions, which he thought were created by his drab routine office work, and he sought clinical intervention to help him to get out of the rut of his dull job and move forward with his life.

In clinical sessions Andrew described the many ways in which he had cut himself off from his family, and he became willing to experiment with reestablishing these contacts as a measure to break down some of the isolation he felt. As his functioning improved, Andrew also explored ways in which religion might take on some degree of meaning for him. A friend introduced him to a New Thought Protestant sect, with a small, enthusiastic, and supportive congregation.

After several visits to this church, Andrew tried to use prayer and meditation as techniques to enlighten and guide his decision making. Within a few weeks he believed that these practices improved the quality of his daily life. After 6 months he was able to rid himself of many of his fears and anxieties, with the result that he was able to select a more meaningful job.

Andrew moved from managing the single office of a small business to working in a local branch of a nationwide bank. After a short period of orientation to his new position, he took advantage of employee tuition benefits by enrolling in courses at a nearby college and signed on for additional on-the-job professional training. Socially, he increased the number of his friends through church contacts, as well as sustained some of his most enjoyable family relationships. He also began to date a young woman from his church, who helped him to clarify his ideas, beliefs, and values through their extended conversations.

Andrew rose to most of the challenges of clinical exchanges and increased his personal, professional, and social successes. Some family members supported his decisions to make these important changes in his life, and Andrew persisted in his rather idiosyncratic patterns of religious worship in spite of his relatives' curiosity and questioning. Having successfully broadened his horizons, Andrew was able to plan effectively for the future.

Analysis

Andrew no longer suffered from depressions once he reestablished contact with several members of his family. Furthermore, he found that communicating with and actually visiting relatives energized him sufficiently to be able to reflect meaningfully about other kinds of changes he could make to break down his isolation and boredom.

When the topic of religious affiliation and beliefs was raised in clinical discussions, Andrew initially reacted with many different kinds of negative feelings. Andrew was convinced that his family's religious beliefs and practices had essentially closed him off from the rest of the world when he was a young boy, and that this estrangement had compounded his symptoms of depression. Consequently, Andrew realized that he would have to change his style of worship, if not the substance of his religious beliefs themselves, if religion were to hold any significance for him.

It is largely because of Andrew's ability to think independently and to be autonomous that his course of therapy was so successful. He worked out some of the specific conflicts he had had with his parents as a child as well as pursued new directions in his life. This emotional resolution helped Andrew to be adventurous in seeking out further education and training in his new position at the bank. His church contacts gave him support as well as friendship, and he found that he genuinely gained a great deal from reviving and reformulating his religious beliefs.

Andrew's spiritual development, together with his new church affiliation, enhanced his efforts to sort out conflicts and contradictions in his interpersonal relationships. Even though he was much more satisfied with his new work than he had been in his former job, he took the time to formulate careful plans to move to other geographical locations in the future; working at a national bank facilitated the coordination of this goal.

The breadth of Andrew's vision, and his positive assessments of career and social possibilities, created high levels of openness and creativity in his daily routines. In spite of his successes, or even because of them, Andrew decided to continue his therapy. However, he scheduled longer and longer intervals between clinical sessions so that he could apply his new principles of daily living at the same time as keep on track with his fairly ambitious, but healthily realistic plans.

STRATEGIES FOR CLINICAL INTERVENTIONS

Professionally and ethically, one of clinicians' primary responsibilities is to place their highest priority on clients' realizations of themselves. This goal must be accomplished in ways that express clients' values, rather than according to clinicians' agendas or needs to experiment with new research hypotheses. Thus, it is crucial to construct clients' identities through examining their views in clinical exchanges. Clinical strategies must place clients center stage to facilitate understanding the meanings and implications of their preferred values and habitual value choices.

When clients are encouraged to consider values in light of their own religious experiences and observations, a wide variety of intense negative reactions may be precipitated (McNamara, 1992). Clinicians must handle these emotions effectively, because discussions about religious preferences can be particularly useful in strengthening clients' identities. Furthermore, these exchanges give clinicians increased opportunity to assess the intensity of clients' religious and secular belief systems, and to gauge ways in which clients may use or abuse religion, or allow themselves to be used or abused by others.

Because clinical exchanges need to be conducted with as high a level of awareness as possible, both clinicians and their clients will benefit from clinicians' recognition of the links between their own identities and religions. When clinicians trace their personal development in relation to religious and secular belief systems, they will become more effective agents of change, and have more substantial impacts on clients' decision making and behavior, than if they did not attain this kind of self-knowledge.

10 Clinical Tasks

1. Take notes on clients' life histories about religious socialization and participation in religious practices.
2. Assess the extent to which religions are important to individual clients.
3. Outline those parts of clients' religious beliefs that seem to mean the most to them.

4. Analyze some of the ways in which clients have internalized their beliefs and values.
5. List those values that seem to be most important to clients.
6. Estimate whether clients express their beliefs and convictions in their daily behavior.
7. Ask clients how they see the influence of religion and values in their lives.
8. Find out which relationships and events formulated, and continue to influence, clients' beliefs.
9. Assess the extent to which clients are interested in making changes in their lives, and which changes they want to make most.
10. Encourage clients to continue to make in-depth analyses of daily expressions of their beliefs and values.

Chapter 4

Society and Religion

The links between society and religion are closer than may appear from mere observation of today's world (Wuthnow, 1992). In fact, cultural evolution, and even the evolution of society itself, have been thought of as depending largely on the institution of religion (Ashbrook, 1993; Durkheim, 1915). For millennia, society has needed religions to create and sustain sufficient degrees of value consensus for the continued existence of communities and society (McGuire, 1994).

Religions not only enhance social sharing through ceremonial rituals and practices, but also exert pressures on individuals to conform to religious norms through applications of both positive and negative sanctions (Durkheim, 1915). These sanctions are extremely powerful for believers, because they are based on sacred authorities rather than on secular laws (Marty & Appleby, 1991). A clear illustration of this phenomenon is found in the past and present experiences of fundamentalists (Bendroth, 1994; Marty & Appleby, 1991).

As societies modernized, some social scientists predicted that religions would lose these influences (Durkheim, 1915). Although it is undoubtedly true that increasing numbers of people modify traditional religious beliefs, in the long run many religions go through revival cycles and thus continue to exert considerable power in society. For instance, fundamentalist Protestant sects have become increasingly influential in the United States throughout the last decade. The sacred lives on in contemporary society, despite the great strength of secularizing influences (Wuthnow, 1992). Furthermore, successful political leaders, such as Reverend Martin Luther King, Jr., are often publicly associated with dominant religious denominations, with the result that important political events may include acknowledgments to specific, largely shared religious beliefs, even though these may be so eclectic that they have been described as civil or secular religions (Kosmin & Lachman, 1993). These kinds of associations of political power and religions also permeate religious organizations in the United States (Beckford & Luckmann, 1989).

Thus, evidence suggests that religion and society are inextricably related to each other through complex evolutionary processes, which pattern social dependencies within and between different cultures (Eisler, 1987). Religions link people to forces that are beyond their daily realities, and both individual and social benefits frequently flow from this relationship, even though there can be mystification rather than liberation through specific religious symbolizations (Kaufman, 1993). It is for these reasons that religions can be fully understood only through examining their social contexts (McGuire, 1994).

SOCIETY AND THE CONCEPT OF GOD

With society as a starting point, it is possible to trace some correlations between social structures and godheads or supernatural powers (Yinger, 1957). When society is complex, modern, and hierarchical, its godheads and supernatural powers reflect its hierarchies and ideals, with a supreme power—for example, God—as the highest point in the social and divine hierarchies (Wuthnow, 1992). By contrast, more egalitarian societies, such as some African agrarian communities, frequently have animistic or polytheistic supernatural powers, which are not hierarchically ordered (Hess, 1991). Thus, societies produce particular forms of religion, and religions reflect particular forms of society (Durkheim, 1915).

In less developed societies, concepts of God or supernatural powers relate more directly to survival and environmental concerns (Hess, 1991). When nature and fertility are vital to a society's survival, symbolic representations of nature and fertility are found in that society's religious worship and rituals (Durkheim, 1915). Thus survival conditions of a particular society are automatically incorporated in that society's religious symbol systems, frequently including a supreme symbol of a godhead (Ashbrook, 1993).

Personal experiences of divine presence may also be conceived as responses to omnipresent societal influences (James, 1969). The divine is often thought of as including everything beyond human comprehension, and therefore representing the overwhelming powers of society and the unknown—that is, powers upon which people ultimately depend for their survival (Ashbrook, 1993). Therefore, societies may be thought of as being essentially worshipped, created, and perpetuated through their religious rituals. For example, totemic beliefs are aimed solely at perpetuating group survival. Religions endure because of their societal bases, and societies endure because of religious practices and shared beliefs in supernatural powers. Protestantism, and Puritanism in particular, served as underpinnings for all rapid technological changes in the United States. Thus the reciprocity between society and its given concept of God is indestructible, explaining why people may experience themselves as being dependent on godheads in some of the same ways in which they are dependent on society.

When praying for guidance, people are addressing the most powerful forces of society, and personal understandings of divine being come into play (Weber, 1958). People gain inspiration from listening to their inner selves, which derive from society as well as from beliefs in supernatural powers. For example, self and society reflect each other in varied cultural settings. Concepts of God represent the essence of society as well as concerns about the unknown, and reflect social origins as well as shared beliefs in divine sources (Durkheim, 1915). Thus, religions have crucial social meanings for individuals and groups, as well as belief systems in their own right (Progoff, 1985).

RELIGION AND SOCIAL CHANGE

Although religions are indisputably sources of great stability in society, and may characteristically resist change, they also provide values and meanings that give purpose and direction to social innovations, even revolutions (Haney, 1989). Contemporary liberation theology in Latin America shows how radical religious thought can precipitate and support social movements that seek to make far-reaching changes (Smith, 1991). Religions have both priestly and prophetic traditions (Weber, 1958). Priestly traditions, such as Roman Catholicism, inspire forms of leadership and worship that embellish and celebrate the status quo; whereas prophetic traditions, such as Protestantism, encourage alternative forms of leadership and worship that promote progress toward increased individual and social freedom.

These two distinctive approaches to reality and change are reinforced through individuals' religious and value choices. The status quo is necessarily celebrated by conforming to ritualistic values, which honor traditional answers to deep human questions about the nature of reality. For example, the long history of church-building in the United States from 1776 to 1990 is evidence of the power of religions' conservative influences (Finke & Stark, 1992). On the other hand, religions that increase freedom and promote change are frequently sectarian rather than denominational, and suggest new interpretations of religious doctrines as well as new revelations. Calvinism inspired some of the early entrepreneurial thinking in the industrial revolution (Weber, 1958), and, more recently, feminist spirituality has promoted visions of change that increase motivations to struggle for justice (Haney, 1989).

Identity and religion are expressed synchronously when individuals receive religious or secular vocations, calls to action. Historical figures such as Martin

Luther illustrate the power of vocation in transforming individual lives and society. It is often through receiving vocations that strongly committed individuals accomplish specific religious or secular goals and have a major impact on society (Weber, 1958). However, because individuals may receive callings to fill particular roles, rather than to achieve goals, vocations can as easily maintain traditions and sustain the status quo as make innovations (Bendroth, 1994). In both cases, however, religions add momentum to individual decision making and behavior, and directly influence the degree of change actually accomplished (Jung, 1933).

Although national policy may separate religions from politics, as in the United States, there are many common denominators and necessary overlaps in religious and political issues at deep levels of values that support the status quo—traditional or modern values that precipitate changes and innovations (Kosmin & Lachman, 1993). However well politics may be purged of religious concerns, or religions kept free from political pressures, these two major social institutions necessarily converge (Haney, 1989). In fact, results from the differences in power of these countervailing influences make up the kinds of social changes experienced. For example, in the United States, overlaps between religious affiliations and political standing are especially evident in the mainstream denominations of Protestantism, Catholicism, and Judaism, and therefore have marked social consequences in relation to the status quo (Herberg, 1955).

Examining issues of religion and social change points up differences between the kinds of changes that human beings can accomplish and those things that cannot be controlled (Haught, 1984). Evolutionary change, for example, is so slow that a human lifetime is minuscule in comparison. Furthermore, given the discrepancies in time frames between evolution and history, religious beliefs appear to have less of an impact on evolutionary changes than on more time-restricted historical shifts, which are also experienced more acutely (Ashbrook, 1993). However, in some respects the human quest for purpose can be considered in relation to evolutionary change, especially when studies of the development of religion, science, and human meaning are examined (Haught, 1984). By contrast, the trials and tribulations of war generally affect each person more dramatically than overall slow-moving environmental influences (Ryan, 1992).

RELIGIOUS SYMBOLS

Symbols distill and concentrate human meanings (Mead, 1934). Religious symbols are cultural or natural objects that point to nonempirical referents, so that their meanings transcend their empirical dimensions, as well as the individual and social implications of these same cultural or natural objects (Yinger, 1957).

Each religion has its own symbols, and some religions have richer symbol systems than others (James, 1969). Thus symbols in different religions, as well as symbols in the same religion, represent a broad range of values (Hechter et al., 1993). However, to the extent that subjective interpretations are necessarily involved in deciphering religious symbols, the substance of symbols' sacred referents necessarily remains fluid (Kaufman, 1993).

Religious symbols may represent or suggest either religious hierarchies or the lack of religious hierarchies. Hinduism, for example, is a pantheon of divinities, whereas Taoism is expressly without such a sacred structure. Although the godheads of religions may not themselves be symbolized—in some belief systems this would be considered idolatrous—rituals and practices around worship of the sacred are usually embellished by distinctive symbol systems (Stark & Glock, 1968). Furthermore, human beings understand the language of symbols and imagery at deep emotional levels rather than intellectually (Jung, 1933). As they respond, or even react, to many different kinds of religious symbols, their emotional receptivity helps to organize believers into communities of worship. For instance, rituals are symbolic observances that build Jewish and Roman Catholic congregations. Religious symbols frequently create certain levels of consensus, if only for creating agreement about the meanings of these symbols (Kosmin & Lachman, 1993; Wuthnow, 1992). In addition to helping to construct religious communities, religious symbols provide purpose and direction for individuals and their belief systems. Life cycle changes and seasons of the year, for example, are incorporated into symbolic cycles in most major religious denominations and sects (Yinger, 1957).

RITES AND ROLES

Practices as well as beliefs are essential aspects of religions. Religious rituals or rites are therefore key components of religious experiences, and may also be thought of as significant units of religious belief systems and religious communities (Lenski, 1961).

For a rite to exist, there has to be sufficient agreement among religious adherents about its specific form, flow, and meaning. Many rites surround major life events such as births, marriages, and deaths, as well as different seasons of the year (James, 1969). In fact, unless religions have particularly sparse symbol systems (as does the Quaker religion), all major life stages and seasonal transitions are usually expressed, supported, and embellished by rites. Furthermore, it is through their ritualistic worship of the sanctity of life and the world that believers most effectively unite (Herberg, 1955).

Rites are necessarily performed by both leaders and followers, and the division of labor in both sacred and secular communities is itself is upheld by rituals of some kind. People are who they are not only through the identities they create, but also by virtue of the roles they are expected to perform. Roles in sacred and secular communities are frequently related to each other, in that one set of roles directly or indirectly supports the other. For example, a rabbi is a teacher in a religious congregation, but may have a higher social status than many other kinds of teachers in secular communities. Thus everyday roles tend to be strongly endorsed by social and religious processes, and devotional or ceremonial rites either restrict or expand people's perspectives and day-to-day situations.

Individuals with strong identities are able to transcend roles that are thrust upon them, thereby neutralizing either the sacred or the secular conventions that support these roles. For example, identity may neutralize the social labels of mother and daughter that can inhibit women. Because traditional roles tend to be arranged in hierarchies, as people modify their roles through strengthening their identities, they simultaneously open up communities to become more egalitarian.

Both religions and spirituality can bridge the known and the unknown, the possible and the impossible (Manuel & Manuel, 1979). Whereas religious rites tend to reinforce established religious and social roles, strengthening identity can neutralize or eliminate some of the restrictiveness of rites and roles. If individuality is maintained as well as participation in community rituals, it is more possible to make contributions to society than either by living in relative isolation or by total submission to social influences (McNamara, 1992).

RELIGION AND COMMUNITY

Religions create communities, whether or not these communities use symbols or practice rituals. In fact, religions are usually defined in terms of communities of believers, even though it is evident that communities are more important in some religions, such as Judaism, than in others, such as Taoism. A religious community necessarily is based on having some explicit shared beliefs and practices, and this specificity of beliefs and practices separates religions from each other and separates religious and secular communities.

Although membership in a particular religious community frequently occurs by default—perhaps by virtue of being born into a family religion—religious beliefs are often professed by a person so as to feel a sense of belonging to a religion or a religious community. Furthermore, it may be difficult to place a priority on the tenets of a particular religion without actually participating in that religion's community. Thus, identifying with certain religious values and ideals makes believers, and sharing religious beliefs with others increases participation in the living consensus of a particular religious community, bestowing membership in that community.

It is in these ways that identification with religious values breaks down isolation and alienation, and allows individuals to be part of the whole of society. For example, in the United States religious symbols serve to achieve national unity as well as religious unity (Kosmin & Lachman, 1993), as in the case of Shintoism in Japan. Experiencing identification with religious beliefs is qualitatively distinct from experiencing separateness from others, which brings with it a lack of responsibility for social outcomes.

The ultimate community of many religions, particularly major world religions, is the entire human race (Ashbrook, 1993). Even though religions may not be expressly universalist in scope, wherever there are hierarchies of values or supernatural powers there are also specific shared assumptions and implications about the nature of human beings, the human condition, and the human race. These underlying premises are powerful determinants of individual and social behavior, as well as of institutional processes and social structures (Berger & Luckmann, 1967).

THE INDIVIDUAL, RELIGION, AND SOCIETY

Realizing moral agency through action facilitates the development of a perspective that connects individuality, values, beliefs, and society at large. The cores of selves are necessarily connected to evolutionary forces, or to the broadest social changes, and these connections create a comprehensive awareness of particular purposes and specific directions for daily living (Hall, 1990a).

Religions can serve as prisms through which to see these linkages (Fromm, 1967). For example, religions frequently encourage individuals to ask deep and serious questions about the nature of reality and the nature of humanity, which may not otherwise be asked. These thoughtful assessments within the context of religions are then based in the broadest possible perspectives of time and place.

Social processes are indescribably and incomprehensibly complex, and these intricacies cannot be understood by examining them in isolation from each other. A worthwhile objective is to understand how individual and social behavior is affected by individuality, religions, and society—religions being focal points in the many interactions between individuals and society. Changes in status and consciousness can be made by using religions to understand relationships and dependencies between the individual and society, as well as to clarify responsibilities of moral agents. Although it is true that both sacred and secular beliefs define identities, such as being a Muslim and being a Democrat, in the long run it is primarily the impetus of the sacred that transcends empirical restrictions in day-to-day situations (Wuthnow, 1992).

SOCIETY AND RELIGION

Society makes use of many religious concepts in its formulations of ideals (McGuire, 1994). Society needs sacred values and beliefs to adapt effectively to evolutionary forces and to the strong, interactive influences of its own basic social institutions. Thus, cultural evolution extends the biological survival of the human species (Ashbrook, 1993; Berger & Luckmann, 1967; Durkheim, 1951).

Insofar as societies need religions to survive, religions also need societies as sources of meaning and arenas of application for their symbol systems (Yinger, 1957). Concepts of godheads and supernatural powers are definitively informed by cultural experiences, and religious rites and rituals are essentially social processes. For example, births, marriages, and deaths are secular events that are sacralized through religious observances and rituals. This intense interdependence of religion and society either precipitates or inhibits social change, within the context of evolutionary development (Smith, 1991; Warner, 1993; Wilson, 1986). Furthermore, although different religious communities may be in conflict with each other, there must be some merging of values for society to survive as an integrated system. Thus, even the most highly differentiated, pluralistic societies have to have some degree of consensus about values, beliefs, and ideals (Durkheim, 1915).

As societies become more secular, as in Western Europe, paradoxically their religions can become both more liberalized and more traditionalized. For example, the secular freedom of France contrasts with the religious restrictiveness of Ireland and Spain. Whereas secularization may have an influential impact on some religious forms and practices, other religions and religious movements resist secularization by becoming more traditional (Marty & Appleby, 1991). Even though religions may be driven underground by modernization or specific political belief systems, as in the former Soviet Union, in the long run these same religions tend to persist and emerge through more routinized adaptations to the whole of society (Kosmin & Lachman, 1993; Wuthnow, 1992).

QUESTIONS AND ANSWERS

To understand some of the complex correlations between identity and religion, a question must be posed: "How close is the relationship between religion and society?" Historically, and from the point of view of evolution, religion served as a base for early communities and simple societies, and has continued to serve as a core of modern-day cultures (Wuthnow, 1992). As a consequence, many social values derive from religious belief systems, and secular cultural and moral standards have developed from the original religious categories of right and wrong, or of sacred and profane (Hechter et al., 1993; Wuthnow, 1992). It is in these respects that social selves are closely related to religion, whether or not these influences are widely acknowledged.

Another question that deepens understanding of religion and society is "What role does religion play in the course of evolutionary adaptation?" From this perspective, it appears that in the earliest stages of human evolution religions facilitated the formation of communities through their shared belief and symbol systems. Religions also anchored social values during times of relatively rapid social change, thus making evolutionary adaptation more viable than radical change of the system itself (Weber, 1958). By sustaining individual and group efforts to adjust to rapid shifts in environmental conditions, religion makes social continuities and societal survival more possible (Ashbrook, 1993). Thus religions guard societies against premature extinction by amplifying and extending social meanings in religious traditions and other socially established ways of doing things (Jung, 1993; Progoff, 1985).

However, as well as having these conserving functions, religions can also precipitate changes by disseminating innovative ideas and increasing motivation to bring about social betterment. Religions cannot be associated solely with stabilizing social forms and processes.

In scrutinizing some of the many ways in which religion impedes or expedites social change, a further question needs to be asked: "How does religion support the status quo?" Although any answers to this question oversimplify real explanations, some patterns can be outlined. For example, the status quo is preserved because religions tend to sacralize given divisions of labor (Durkheim, 1915). These crucially significant patterns of interaction are perpetuated through religious sanctions, which encourage particular groups of people to continue to perform socially expected roles and functions.

An essential and responsible task of individuals with strong identities is to challenge sacralized traditional models of status and behavior. Thus, through strengthening identity, both individuals and collectives can work with concerted effort to modify socially authorized patterns of behavior that would otherwise be supported and perpetuated by religions.

GENERALIZATIONS

A key generalization is that religion and society are closely interrelated, whether or not they are recognized to be so, and that patterns of behavior and substantive values characterizing particular religions are reflections of broad social trends. Furthermore, individuals can become more integrated with society by incorporating religious values into their interactions and commitments.

Religions build consensus, because they are largely defined by their shared values. Thus, religions frequently increase social cohesiveness and agreement in societies. This is a particularly useful function, because shared values form the core of all cultures, whether or not these cultures are religious. In societies where religions thrive and function effectively, degrees of consensus about definitions of good and evil, or about standards of right and wrong, may be greater than in societies where religions do not thrive. Religions enhance the probability of having a viable consensus in society, which itself enhances society's survival, however diverse and pluralistic the religions and societies may be.

Both social sanctions and secular authorities have generally developed from religious sources. Because, historically, religions formed the bases of the earliest communities, social hierarchies developed in relation to hierarchies of sacred and profane values (Durkheim, 1915). Even though religious standards of right and wrong may be assimilated by secular cultures, their social origins remain religious.

Another example of the interplay between society and religion is that concepts of supernatural powers and religious belief systems frequently reflect social hierarchies. Symbolizations of how supernatural powers are defined necessarily reflect a population's understanding of the nature of the universe. Similarly, individual and social identities reflect this high level of interdependence between society and religion.

PROPOSITIONS

Because human beings are socialized, their identities are necessarily strongly influenced by religious realities, such as varied belief systems, symbols, rituals, positive and negative sanctions, authority figures, and concepts of supernatural forces. Moreover, because of the inextricable closeness between religion and society, individual fulfillment and social well-being are also closely related.

Even though societies become increasingly pluralistic as they evolve, their patterns of differentiation have religious sources and bases. Also, cultures continue to have religious cores, in spite of the coexistence of complex secularization and diversification processes. Societal consensus is a necessary component for evolutionary adaptation, and religions are a significant source of that consensus.

Where religions are more uniform and less diverse, religious rites and roles, as well as religious sanctions that support conventional divisions of labor, are correspondingly more clearly demarcated. Where religions are less uniform and more diverse, religious rites and roles, as well as religious sanctions that support conventional divisions of labor, are less clearly demarcated. However, even the most secular social conditions, from the point of view of evolution, are characterized by complex moral and ethical concerns, because both social values and secular cultures derive from religious sources.

Religious symbols may mystify rather than clarify social awareness, and may motivate behavior either to preserve social forms or to innovate through developing new processes. Religious symbols provide meanings that help people deal with social realities and time, and they are therefore means of successful adaptation in rapidly changing societies.

CHOICES

One choice for individuals is either to honor or deny the closeness of religion and society through decision making and behavior. Honoring the closeness of religion and society necessarily increases enlightened action, whereas denying this association results in decreasing meaning and effectiveness. Thus both social well-being and levels of productivity flow from world views and the ways in which decisions are made (Strunk, 1979).

Participation in specific religious denominations or religious sects is not as significant to individuals' functioning as gaining meaning from religious values, whatever their structural context. Both denominational and sectarian values can strengthen motivation to bring about both individual and social changes. People choose whether particular religions are salient to them on the basis of their meaningfulness. However, even though this decision has a major impact on behavior, as well as on perceptions of social circumstances, the substance of different religions does not define destinies as much as does consistency in everyday expressions of values through behavior.

Religious values are chosen as sources of either mystification or enlightenment, and such choices determine whether particular values bring about constructive or destructive consequences. Even though religions frequently sanction certain authority figures, the choice remains of whether to accept these influences. When ways in which authority is grounded in religious traditions are known, these choices become freer and more meaningful.

In the case study that follows, religious influences on both society and the perception of oneself are explored.

CASE STUDY

Helen Weiss was an upper-middle-class, single Jewish woman from a tightly knit Eastern European Jewish family. She was raised to have different career ideas from those of her three brothers, even though her parents paid for her to attend a local college. Her parents wanted Helen to get married, have a family, and settle down near them.

As a child Helen had been overwhelmed by patriarchal dominance in her family, as well as the patriarchal characteristics of Judaism. She sought therapy to strengthen her self-esteem, and to help her to decide what she wanted to do with her life. She had no close attachments with men friends and had no intentions of marrying until she had developed her career. She hoped that therapy would help her to deal with her parents and three brothers while she sorted out her priorities.

One ambition Helen had, which she had nurtured since childhood, was to become a rabbi, even though—and perhaps because—she had suffered restrictions from her religious heritage. Her goal of becoming a rabbi ran counter to her parents' expectations and brothers' views of her. However, Helen believed in education and wanted to make Judaism a more hospitable place for women by becoming a leader in a congregation.

Helen's course of therapy supported her choice of vocation and served to give her a clearer sense of who she was in the context of contemporary society. This vantage point strengthened Helen's position in relation to her family and helped persuade her parents to contribute financially to her quest for more education and professional studies. Because some of the family's local synagogue members also supported Helen, her parents agreed to go along with this plan, at least provisionally.

Once this career decision was made and recognized by her family, Helen's life began to open up socially. Helen easily made more women friends in her religious community, as well as at the new university she attended, and she became more sensitized to women's issues as well as her professional studies.

She worked on increasing her network of women friends and colleagues, and tried to make men friends who were interested in feminist ideas.

Analysis

Helen had a successful outcome of therapy because she was able to be single-minded in her pursuit of further study and career development. Her professional goal and social contacts helped her to withstand some of the family criticism she received, and she became motivated to change some of her patterns of dependence in her family relationship system.

Helen became less overwhelmed and discouraged by the patriarchal tendencies in her home and religion, and she strengthened her personal mission to further women's interests and concerns within Judaism. A related decision was that she became sufficiently freed up to join a Reform Jewish congregation and pursue Reform rabbinical studies, even though she had been raised as a Conservative Jew. This move strengthened her autonomy in relation to her parents and brothers, and she became able to explore and discover which particular aspects of Judaism she wanted to study. She was interested in the historical roots of Reform Judaism, and the principle of progressive revelation motivated her to find new answers to pressing contemporary social and religious concerns.

STRATEGIES FOR CLINICAL INTERVENTIONS

Ideally, clinical interventions should be based on a good working knowledge of the reciprocity of influences between religion and society. This knowledge can be achieved through observations, experiences, and examinations of substantive research findings (Poloma & Gallup, 1991). Understanding these correlations increases awareness of some of the moral dilemmas individuals face as they cope with difficult situations (Smith, 1987). Clinicians who can define some of the ways in which clients' personal troubles are influenced by religion and society become more adept at encouraging those clients to become freer in their own rights than if they did not have this working knowledge.

Understanding both the explicit and implicit functions of religion in society means that clinicians need to recognize religious influences even when they are not obviously present as particular belief systems, rites, or practices. For example, moral judgments derive from a variety of religious sources, and individuals adhere to particular standards of right and wrong in large part because of the emotional tone of the religious beliefs held by significant others in their immediate social contexts. A professional perspective that takes these different influences into account improves the long-term effectiveness of clinical interventions.

Another helpful technique for gaining knowledge about religious influences is for clinicians to note and understand the tenacity with which clients hold their everyday beliefs. Degrees of intensity and closure of religious beliefs are directly related to the kinds of assumptions people make about human nature and the universe. These definitions of ultimate reality have profound influences on clients' behavior, as well as deep roots in both religious and secular cultures (Beckford & Luckmann, 1989).

Even though this kind of analysis is complex, it is more viable for clinicians to consider the depth and strength of social influences in their clients' moral decision making than solely to analyze clients' feelings, especially when feelings are inherently difficult to assess or even name. Whereas the task of scrutinizing feelings is necessarily unending, moral choices and ethical dilemmas can be understood to some extent when they are viewed in specific contexts that highlight the interdependency of individuals, religion, and society, such as families. Also, because people are themselves largely products of the moral decisions they make, clinical work must account for the significance of value influences in clients' everyday lives.

This kind of focus in clinical interventions is further sharpened by discussions about clients' identities and value choices. Changing modes of clients' decision making from being destructive in their consequences to being constructive is an important contributor to clinical progress, individual growth, and personal development. The basic value choice of encouraging a client to make self-development the highest priority in daily activity becomes a significant orientation for additional value choices. Paradoxically, making value choices to strengthen the self ultimately leads to choosing values that honor the well-being of others.

To the extent that clients have grown out of immediate, compelling crises and are sufficiently at ease to be able to see themselves in broad social contexts, they will be able to make more advantageous value choices for themselves and others. For this reason, focusing clinical discussions on self, religion, and society can be a constructive therapeutic base for clinical interventions, leading to more effective clinical outcomes than could narrower starting points.

10 Clinical Tasks

1. Discover how clients respond to symbolizations of their own religious beliefs.

2. Examine the extent to which clients see themselves as members of specific religious communities.
3. Outline the status of clients in relation to formal religious organizations.
4. Assess how religions have influenced clients' roles in religions and society.
5. Determine how religions influence clients' world views.
6. Assess whether clients follow priestly or prophetic traditions in their religious observances.
7. Take histories of how clients incorporate religious and secular values in their lives.
8. Discuss why clients see religion as precipitating or impeding social change.
9. Estimate how clients relate to religious rituals.
10. Encourage clients to step outside their particular religious experiences and assess their relationship to the social institution of religion.

Chapter 5

Families and Religion

People are usually socialized into religions by their families rather than through any kind of divine or even social intervention (Lenski, 1961). In fact, for many, lifelong religious affiliations and beliefs result from being ascribed at birth rather than achieved. People tend to follow the religious teachings of parents and grandparents, especially when these relatives share one religion. In these respects religious beliefs—at least in origin—are essentially family products. This fact suggests that the intensity with which beliefs are held is usually more strongly influenced by significant others' degrees of religiosity than by the actual substance of the beliefs (Johnson, 1973).

Individual identities are also strongly influenced by family dynamics; family interdependencies frequently determine which values are internalized and the intensity with which they are internalized. For example, a child is more likely to choose to study engineering if other family members have been engineers. It is only by becoming more autonomous in thinking, decision making, and behavior that individuals are able to neutralize these kinds of family pressures sufficiently to make truly independent choices of values and religious beliefs possible (Hall, 1991).

Religious denominations such as Roman Catholicism and Judaism frequently endorse traditional or conventional family roles and responsibilities (Bendroth, 1994; Marty & Appleby, 1991). Furthermore, religious dictates may make it difficult for individuals to strengthen their identities in relation to family pressures, because religious sanctions are experienced as strong pressures to conform to conventional expectations (Bowen, 1978). However, religious observances that consist largely of communion with supernatural powers are more likely to support individuals, groups, and society in liberating themselves from family traditions and conventions (McNamara, 1992; Mol, 1978).

Religions need families to recruit and train their new members, and many religious communities are largely composed of families. Thus families constitute a significant number of the most powerful religious influences on individuals, especially during their formative years. The fact that such a close connection exists between families and religion has important implications for why and how autonomous identities can be created and sustained through value choices (Hall, 1990a, 1991).

FAMILIES AND BELIEFS

Families have their own subcultures of values, some of which are religious, especially where families are devout in their religious practices. Thus families develop specific kinds of sacred and secular belief systems, expectations, and sanctions through time (Johnson, 1973).

The beliefs that make up families' subcultures are more compelling if they originate in religions rather than in secular sources, because religious beliefs are accompanied by powerful sanctions. For example, a significant consequence for family belief systems with religious sources is that dominant family members, typically fathers or grandfathers, may employ religious sanctions to uphold their power and authority. As a result, these dominant family members are experienced as being extremely powerful by dependent family members (Fromm, 1967).

When family belief systems are relatively closed to new ideas and external influences, as beliefs systems in many splintered or itinerant families tend to be, individual family members find it correspondingly difficult to create their own identities. However, the same processes that go into strengthening identities may also serve to modify or open up closed family belief systems. Optimally, family belief systems are open rather than closed; openness allows family members to express their authentic, individual identities more freely.

When dependencies in family relationships shift, family belief systems also change. For example, after the death of a parent an adult child may look to a new religion for comfort and support. Likewise, when family belief systems change, family relationships shift. This reciprocity is such that specific family structures generate particular belief systems, and particular belief systems produce specific family structures. For example, when families are egalitarian and symmetrical rather than hierarchical, as when both parents are equal partners, their belief systems are correspondingly more flexible. When family belief systems are open and flexible, their structures are egalitarian and symmetrical rather than hierarchical (Durkheim, 1915).

In the grand scheme of things, families and religions play essential roles in societies' survival and their effective cultural adaptations. At best, family belief systems orient individual family members toward working for established, socially acceptable goals. In situations where individual beliefs contrast with family beliefs, for example in valuing educational achievement, more innovations and changes result.

RELIGIONS AND FAMILY ROLES

When religions define family roles in traditional and conservative ways, they essentially restrict the range of choices individuals may make to create their identities. For example, historically religions have played conservative roles in silencing women, as religious conditioning virtually coerced women to define their primary moral responsibilities as meeting family members' needs through unpaid labor (Erickson, 1993). However, if religions are practiced through prayer, meditation, and relationships with godheads, rather than through rituals that merely perpetuate specific community or family roles, these practices may culminate in creative and innovative behavior. Thus religions can inspire and empower people to transcend or modify conventional family roles, and strong identity can reverse conventional influences and neutralize stereotypes (Hall, 1990b).

Another important aspect of reciprocity between religions and family roles is how religions define spousal and parental responsibilities. Although generalizations cannot be made about the specific content of family roles, which are usually variously defined by different religions (Hussain, 1984), an examination of family roles reveals the tenacity with which beliefs defining traditional family roles are held, including definitions of women's and men's responsibilities (Bendroth, 1994; Stoltenberg, 1989).

Identity concerns in relation to religion and family roles include maintaining sufficient options—for both women and men—so that people can be more than their roles, and especially more than their cultural family roles (Hall, 1990a). Parents are more effective, for example, when they think of themselves as whole persons, rather than as role-players (Pollner, 1989). Consequently, for individuals to achieve well-being and creativity in society, there must be modifications rather than just replications of the role prescriptions passed down from generation to generation (Collins, 1990). Promise for the future lies in developing flexible family roles and other kinds of innovations in relation to religion (Chopp, 1989; Stark & Bainbridge, 1985).

FAMILY RESPONSIBILITIES

Sometimes it is easier to see the effects of the moral power of religions in defining family responsibilities by examining less familiar religions, for example (for Westerners), Islam (Hussain, 1984). Responsibility necessarily entails moral choices, and religions tend to sanction positively those family responsibilities that sustain traditional gender divisions of labor and traditional gender roles (Durkheim, 1951). However, if religious experiences result more from relationships between individuals and godheads or supreme powers than from religious community pressures, family responsibilities may be defined in more flexible ways, which can meet individual preferences as well as community needs. If their religion suggests that people have equal spiritual capacities as children of God, for example, people can be expected to seize sufficient freedom to take more balanced approaches to considering and accepting their family duties and obligations (Randour, 1993).

One guide to understanding and defining family responsibilities in a comprehensive way is to see and respond to family members as whole persons rather than as parts of relationships. Being responsible for the self and others without being over- or underresponsible is important, because being either over- or underresponsible is the same as being irresponsible (Bowen, 1978).

Imbalances in relationships and families occur if family responsibilities are defined separately from individual identities and empowerment. Trying to help others can create dilemmas in that dependency may be encouraged; also, attempting to meet family members' needs increases the probability of ignoring one's own personal needs (Wuthnow, 1991). Ideally, actions must be synchronized so that a strengthening and empowering of both self and others can occur, rather than a heightening of dependencies through over- or underresponsibility (Hall, 1990a).

INDIVIDUALS AND FAMILIES

Families may be defined as the most intense emotional systems that have existed throughout human evolution, because there is a higher degree of interdependency among family members than among members of any other groups (Bowen, 1978). Freudian thought and psychoanalysis suggest the strength of family influences in defining quality of life and highlight concerns about intensities in family relatedness, because many people are more dependent upon their families than upon other groups (Fromm, 1967).

Although family relationships may be valued and enjoyed, family interdependencies frequently do not inspire independent thinking or meaningful commitments, but rather reactivity and shared needs to survive as a group. Families frequently seek togetherness in their thinking more than independent criticism, for example. By extension, it is sometimes problematic for individuals to extricate themselves sufficiently from their family dependencies to act as autonomous moral agents. However, some degree of autonomy must be achieved for individuals to develop identity (Hall, 1990a).

Identity can be created and nurtured most effectively by considering who each person is in relation to several generations of family members. In fact, it is only through interacting with many different family members at various generational levels that a full understanding of the self can be achieved, and possibilities for continued growth defined. When personal interests and characters are developed in the contexts of families or significant others' relationship systems, growth can be sustained over longer periods of time.

RELIGIONS NEED FAMILIES

As well as needing families to recruit new members into their belief systems, religions need families' presence and participation in community rites and practices (Johnson, 1973). To the extent that an essential defining characteristic of most religions is community worship, families are important constituencies of religious communities.

A variety of religious rituals are designated for major family events and life turning points, such as births, marriages, and deaths. For example, families look toward religions for support and meaning at times of great rejoicing or sadness. Seasons of individual and family life cycles are sanctified by religions through varied annual, seasonal, weekly, and even daily rites and practices. In these ways religions create a felt, dramatic presence, which becomes a significant reality for many families.

Although religions establish and perpetuate family needs for religions, it is doubtful that families need religions with the degree of urgency or dependency that religions need families. Because families directly reproduce their members, they can survive over time rather than become extinct. By contrast, religions cannot create new members alone, so they are forced to cooperate closely with families to meet their membership needs (Erickson, 1993). Recognizing this imbalance in the frequently symbiotic relationship between families and religion makes it possible for both individuals and families to become freer of religious demands (Randour, 1993).

It can therefore be surmised that, although religions need families and some families need religions, family members can break through this interdependency to sustain more flexible and individualistic bonds with religions, for example through their devotional practices. Furthermore, it is particularly through identity formulations and identity empowerment that religions can support or inspire, rather than restrict or limit individual and social behavior (Hall, 1986a, 1986b, 1991).

FAMILIES, RELIGIONS, AND ADAPTATION

Both families and religions are primary social institutions that serve as foundations for other kinds of social organizations, such as the economic and political systems. Both families and religions also influence behavior profoundly at emotional levels, with the result that even though the content and processes of religions and families sometimes run counter to human intellect and reason, they continue to have compelling influences over behavior. For example, women's spirituality and other kinds of nontraditional religious expressiveness have significant secular or political consequences, because the motivating and mobilizing powers of religious beliefs can be manifested in many different kinds of social behavior (Spretnak, 1982).

Similarly, what goes on in families and religions has direct consequences for society at large. Because individuals and societies adapt to broad evolutionary forces through their social institutions, when these social institutions are balanced society is more stable than when relationships among them are not harmonious (Hall, 1981). The five basic social institutions found in most societies are family, religion, the economy, education, and the political system, and, although families and religions are distinctive in that they meet some of human beings' deepest emotional needs, it is important to consider relationships among all five of these social institutions to assess the degrees of synchrony and effectiveness of adaptation in any given society accurately. Adaptation cannot be taken for granted; sufficient imbalance among social institutions eventually leads to societal extinction. The interdependence among the five basic social institutions was recently illustrated through the social consequences of the collapse of the former Soviet Union and some Eastern European countries.

Although individual decision making may seem remote from the broad scale of social institutions and evolution, all human actions are interrelated, and these kinds of microcosms of the whole are crucial links in chains of social being. Thus, individual value choices, and their resulting individual and social adaptations, are integral parts of overall institutional and societal adaptations. Clearly developed individual and group identities move people more forcefully in directions of progress or constructive evolutionary changes than less well-defined identities (Teilhard de Chardin, 1965). Because strengthening identities predictably increases contributions to society, those values that promote stronger identities predictably become components of societywide cultural processes.

Consensus and culture are living phenomena that lead toward either adaptation or extinction, and it is only when identities cultivate constructive collective values that society's adaptation is predictably ensured (Ashbrook, 1993; Jung, 1933).

FAMILIES AND RELIGIOUS REINFORCEMENTS

Families frequently turn to religious sources for support and reinforcement, either as groups or as individuals (Ellison, 1991; Hunsberger, 1985; Pargament et al., 1988; Pollner, 1989). Clinical research documents the potential problem-solving functions of religions as well as ways in which religions serve as coping mechanisms and sources of support (Pargament et al., 1988). When neither denominational nor sectarian beliefs are meaningful, however, these traditional beliefs can be modified by developing spirituality (Randour, 1993).

Although many spiritual beliefs have religious origins, spiritual beliefs are frequently more focused on everyday applications, and on individual communications with a supreme power, than on traditional or conventional ritualistic observances (Spretnak, 1982). However, in one way or another, both religions and spirituality may serve as sources of strength in times of need. For example, religious and spiritual resources enable family members to transcend their interpersonal problems, and may provide ways out of individual and social entrapments resulting from a variety of family dysfunctions.

At a minimum, religious and spiritual beliefs provide sanctions and reinforcements for conventional definitions of reality, thereby maintaining the status quo. Thus, even though religious and spiritual influences are often invisible, they are powerful determinants of individual and social behavior. Religions and spirituality provide vitally important, influential views of human nature and the world at large, as well as serve as means for defining religious and secular vocations, missions, and goals (Chopp, 1989).

Many families may participate only superficially in religious rituals and have few expressly spiritual beliefs (Johnson, 1973). However, even with minimal involvement in formal and informal religious observances, religions frequently draw families into their communities, and in the long run may integrate those family members' beliefs with the beliefs of a particular denomination or sect. For example, nonreligious parents may send their children to religious school and later become religious themselves. Thus religious communities and spiritually based groups can provide anchors or homes to those whose beliefs can become congruent with their own (Herberg, 1955).

Individual family members can benefit from incorporating religious and spiritual values into their identities, in that religions and spirituality can provide family members with ideals to guide and direct them in their everyday decisions and behavior. For example, a belief in truth may motivate actions toward further education and professional development. It is in these respects that religious beliefs and values may have lasting impact on the quality of life of family members and society at large (Hunsberger, 1985).

QUESTIONS AND ANSWERS

Two questions put identity and religion into a comprehensive and realistic context: "To what extent do families define religious beliefs?" and "In which ways do religions depend on families?" These questions highlight nuances in the interdependence between families and religions in society at large. Examinations of how people become religious—for example, through their initial family socialization—and how religions recruit their members—for example, through family worship and sacralizations of births, marriages, and deaths—show the closeness and intensity of the innumerable transactions and negotiations that take place between families and religions. These patterns are clear indicators of the interdependence between families and religions, which consists of both sides' particular needs and functions in society at large (Hall, 1981).

Another significant question to ask about families and religion is "Does religion endorse only traditional or conventional family roles and responsibilities?" Because religions incorporate many traditional values, it seems logical to suppose that they inevitably support roles and structures that accommodate established ways of doing things (Lenski, 1961). However, if religions have the potential to innovate and create constructive changes in social processes, they can also play a significant part in defining innovative and creative family roles and responsibilities (Martin, 1990). In fact, when this issue is examined in a moral or ethical light, it may be deemed more responsible to link specific religious values to creating new family roles than to repeat traditional patterns of family relationships, especially in light of contemporary family needs to adapt or respond meaningfully to rapid social changes (Chopp, 1989; Stoltenberg, 1989).

Another significant question is "If spirituality influences and is influenced by relationships between families and religions, does spirituality have a more or less positive influence on individual autonomy and identity than religion?" Whereas religion frequently encourages conformity to established rites and practices, spirituality tends to increase individual autonomy, as well as to strengthen capacities to interpret personal communion with supernatural powers (Randour,

1993; Roof, 1992). Also, spirituality develops and thrives more readily in relation to autonomy and individuality, which are themselves consolidated through personal interpretations (Hammond, 1992). Thus spirituality can be thought of as opening up some of the relatively intense dependencies between families and religion (McNamara, 1992; Mol, 1978). Furthermore, both spiritual values and religious values have the same kind of lasting impact on the quality of life of those who identify with them (Hall, 1990a).

GENERALIZATIONS

Some of the most basic generalizations to be made about families and religion include the principle that family interdependencies are an extremely strong influence on value choices. Even though people may have an intellectual understanding of themselves as free moral agents, much of their behavior is reactive, and their automatic reactions result largely from the conditioning they received through their family emotional systems (Bowen, 1978).

One positive influence that families can have on their members' religious experiences is that they can help strengthen individuals' beliefs and identities by providing rich opportunities for interactions with significant others. Families are very useful and effective arenas for making interpersonal changes and for receiving reinforcements, and because of their emotional intensity families have more powerful influences over their members than other social groups. These effects are largely because of the persistence of particular patterns of behavior through time, especially those that occur across several generations. People can truly benefit when they discover ways to capitalize on their family relationships by becoming more autonomous as they shift their functioning positions (Bowen, 1978).

To the extent that religions sacralize major family life events such as births, marriages, and deaths, they remain closely linked to other kinds of family dynamics. Religions sustain family relationships and integrate them into broader communities. Thus families are both supported and legitimated through religious and moral influences, and family members develop particular standards in their exchanges and transactions by following selected dictates from religious or spiritual ideals, as well as community moral principles.

Religions are significant catalysts for strengthening motivations. They also frequently extend family cultures, and directly or indirectly promote particular value preferences. In addition, individual family members benefit from broadening their horizons and expanding their minds as they cultivate their own particular views of religions and religious world views (Hall, 1986b).

PROPOSITIONS

From some of the foregoing discussions and observations it can be postulated that family dependencies largely determine the quality of religious experiences that individual family members have, as well as the kinds of identities that family members develop. The more autonomous family members are, the more likely they are to select values that both strengthen their functioning positions and give purpose or meaning to their day-to-day activities. Furthermore, dysfunctional families generally have intense, problematic interdependencies, which make members' selections of values from their religious experiences more difficult and less viable. If people from dysfunctional families want to improve the quality of their religious or spiritual experiences, this goal is accomplished most directly by first increasing their autonomy from family dependencies. Strengthened functioning positions are necessarily accompanied by increased selectivity in value choices, with corresponding increases in productive behavior.

Even though families can be effective means for strengthening and freeing the self, many people experience entrapment in family dependencies rather than liberation. Being trapped in family dependencies may block the achievements of autonomy necessary for making value choices that represent real interests. Religions can enhance identities, thereby counteracting stultifying influences and opening up these powerful emotional systems. Accurate family analyses and shifts in family dependencies are essentially preconditions for effective individual functioning, which itself is a precondition for making appropriate value choices to strengthen identity. Religions can serve as rich resources for value choices only when some degree of autonomy within family systems has already been achieved (Malony & Southard, 1992).

CHOICES

People need to choose their overall priorities carefully so as to assume their responsibilities as historical actors. Achieving the strongest functioning positions possible facilitates selection of the most appropriate values for creating meaningful identities. Thus, because levels of functioning are directly affected by the nature of dependencies in family emotional systems, it is essential to pay attention to these dynamics to build strong identities.

Responding constructively to patterns of interaction throughout family systems by becoming more autonomous increases freedom of choice. The capacity to strengthen identity through value choices is contingent on emotional freedom from family pressures and expectations. Functioning autonomously in families facilitates the most constructive choices among values and religious experiences.

The case study that follows explores the relationship of family and religion. Establishing autonomy in family relationships increases the kinds of choices that can be made about prayer, meditation, and other religious or spiritual practices. Similarly, strengthening spiritual capacity increases the kinds of modifications that can be made in conventional or traditional expectations about family roles and responsibilities. Thus individual and social responsibilities are increased through modifying social dictates that affect functioning and value choices.

CASE STUDY

David Green, an Orthodox Jew, sought family therapy because he was considering marriage to a Roman Catholic woman. David was a successful lawyer with a first-rate education and was thereby filling the dreams and ambitions of his doting parents.

Although David had led a very sheltered upper-middle-class life, the elder of two sons living in a suburb, he was sensitive to social issues and the many needs of less privileged people. He had fallen in love with Monica, a nurse, who spent several hours a week volunteering professional assistance to poor families in the inner city.

David was very concerned that his family had reacted negatively to his plans to marry. He was surprised at the intensity with which his parents resisted his decision, and he began to see patterns in his family's behavior only after he started therapy. Knowledge of the interpersonal dependencies in his family system helped David to become more detached and to move on with his life, rather than become inhibited through his desires to please his parents.

David continued to honor his Orthodox Jewish religion, and at the same time he tried to understand why Monica felt excluded from this part of his life. Although he was not prepared to change his religious observances because of what became his official engagement and coming marriage, he did not expect Monica to change her habitual Roman Catholic devotions, either.

David's family continued to disapprove of his engagement, but his parents were somewhat reassured that he had resolved not to modify his own religious observances. David tried to negotiate with Monica to have their future children raised as Jews, but agreement on this point was difficult and the issue remained unresolved, even though they continued to plan their marriage.

Analysis

David needed emotional support during this difficult decision-making period. His therapy sessions provided guidance and an overview of the issues he was dealing with, as well as personal encouragement. David had not had many women friends in his adult life, and he cared deeply for Monica. However, he was also aware of the recent high intermarriage rates within Judaism, and rationally he would have chosen not to marry a woman who was not Jewish. His present situation therefore had created much inner turmoil for him.

David's compromise in this intense situation was to abide by his own religious practices and at the same time move ahead with his engagement and plans to marry Monica. Although David wanted Monica to agree to raise their children as Jews, she was not able to make this decision at this point in time. In spite of this lack of clarity, David wanted to remain engaged and continued to try to persuade Monica.

Although Monica was not accepted by David's family, David was able to stay on track with his own priorities and beliefs. His practices of Judaism were very different from his parents' observances, and he was also able to sustain his distinctiveness in religious worship within the closeness of his relationship with Monica.

David also resigned himself to the fact that, if Monica could not be persuaded to raise their children as Jews, he could still go ahead with their marriage and educate his children to understand and value Orthodox Jewish culture and beliefs. David cared deeply for Monica and was convinced that the values they shared would give them a sound basis for a good marriage and family life.

David's clinical work was successful because he was able to formulate and pursue his own goals, regardless of external pressures from his parents and from Monica. He needed the clinical exchanges to help him to see the whole context of his interpersonal stresses more clearly, and when he did he was able to make significant decisions. He spent time alone to assess his situation and his progress, and was able to move forward toward his long-term goals of a happy marriage with children, together with continuing in his observances of Orthodox Judaism.

STRATEGIES FOR CLINICAL INTERVENTIONS

When clinicians acknowledge the close associations and interdependencies among family emotional systems, religious experiences, and value choices they become more effective change agents. A fuller and more comprehensive understanding also allows clinicians to develop more meaningful and more accurate theoretical perspectives to guide clinical interventions. Because specific strategies and techniques depend on the kind of theoretical assumptions made, clinicians strengthen their functioning and professional capacities when they articulate—at least to themselves—what these assumptions are.

Optimal clinical strategies for crisis interventions focus on improving family functioning as a prerequisite for making effective value choices to build strong identities. However, even though strengthened family functioning is necessary for strengthening identity, it is not sufficient. Clinical discussions still need to focus on the value choices clients make in this process. Although more clinical success is realized when family functioning is definitely improved, religion and spirituality remain valuable resources for value choices in clinical interventions at any stage of personal development.

Historically, traditional clinical disciplines have tended to underestimate the effects of religion and religious beliefs on clients' behavior (Fromm, 1967). Similarly, scant attention has been paid to the positive behavioral consequences of value choices that derive from religious or spiritual sources. Therefore, it seems particularly appropriate for contemporary clinicians to add this dimension of social awareness for their serious consideration and practice while formulating progressive strategies for clinical interventions (Randour, 1993). Because family functioning and religious choices are inextricably related, it is beneficial to scrutinize this interdependence in a wide variety of clinical and social settings to meet clients' specific needs (Schumaker, 1992).

One consideration in taking clients' family histories is to include reports from as many adult members of the same family as possible (Bowen, 1978). Varied family members' observations and viewpoints increase the possibility that clinicians can be objective and accurate in their assessments of patterns of family interaction and of the intensity of family dependencies. The clearer the understanding clinicians have of their clients' worlds, especially of their family contexts, the more effective clinicians can be as change agents.

Ideally, family histories should include details about geographical and occupational locations of three generations of family members, as well as of any marked emotional alliances and cutoffs. Seeing clients as participants in extended family systems is a critical preliminary for assessing the quality of clients' participation in religions, spirituality, and broader society.

10 Clinical Tasks

1. Take detailed family histories of clients, and include reports from as many members of the same family as possible.

2. Ask clients to give information about conflict and distance in their patterns of family interaction through several generations.
3. List the major events that have occurred in clients' family histories: job changes, deaths, geographical moves, etc. Also note correlations between these events and levels of family functioning.
4. Link family dependency patterns to emotional influences in religious socialization.
5. Determine who the moral leaders in families are, as well as the extent of their influences on clients and other family members.
6. Ask clients to describe the moral and social expectations for women and men in their families.
7. Discuss ways in which clients can be themselves, or not, in family contexts.
8. Analyze how families influence clients' definitions of situations, reference groups, and world views.
9. Determine to what extent religion is a determining influence in patterns of clients' family interaction and social behavior.
10. Explore clients' family reactions to deaths of family members, and use this information as evidence of family dependencies in planning for future action.

Chapter 6

Gender and Religion

It is popularly believed that religions offer a life of the spirit to all (James, 1969). However, it is not true that women and men are equals in religions, because women and men do not have similarly sacralized lives, or the same access to supernatural powers, in many religions (Chopp, 1989; Daly, 1968). Certainly, some strides have been made as women have become priests and rabbis in some faiths. However, recent research has substantiated that women continue to have unequal access to godheads in modern industrialized societies, as they did in many preliterate societies; that disproportionately few women lead contemporary religious organizations; and that these patterns in women's distance from sources of religious powers are correlated with perpetuations of women's lower status (Chopp, 1989; Eisler, 1987; Lerner, 1986).

Examinations of gender stereotypes need to be linked to understanding how religions block thinking about gender, restrict individual and social planning, and inhibit everyday life (Daly, 1968). A comprehensive view is required to focus clearly on the influence of established religions in stereotyping expectations for women (Daly, 1968; Spretnak, 1982). Even concepts of good and evil reflect cultural stereotypes of femininity and masculinity in some respects, and there are thought to be significant social consequences—for both women and men—of calling God "He" and "Father" in Western society (Bendroth, 1994).

The extraordinary powers of religions influence many of the ways in which women and men see each other (Hussain, 1984). For example, historically women have been more associated with symbols of evil or temptation to sin than men. Furthermore, what people believe are religious dictates often have stronger impacts on their behavior than the views or pressures of families and friends (Ebaugh, 1993). If these forces conflict, individuals must decide whether to cultivate the sacred or the profane in everyday life (Randour, 1993).

Religious devotions reinforce or challenge gender expectations in many different ways (Erickson, 1993). For example, some religions exaggerate secular evils by imposing restrictions on women's social behavior through their devotional practices (Ebaugh, 1993). Individuals are not separate from their genders, and as gendered beings they need to recognize deep levels of reality that are not apparent to all (Collins, 1990). To some extent this kind of awareness can be realized by practicing religions that both promise and deliver increases in social rewards such as improved health or better functioning (Hunsberger, 1985). To the extent that women can improve their efficiency or well-being through religious or spiritual practices, religions can be considered a constructive resource for women.

To the extent that formal religious affiliations determine social class memberships, gender also influences this correlation (Ryan, 1992). In fact, gender can be thought of as a type of social class, with women and men frequently having contrasting rather than similar religious experiences (Lorentzen, 1991). Even when women and men do not form clearly recognizable separate social classes with their own distinctive circumstances or beliefs, gender biases in religions may polarize them (Ryan, 1992). However, optimally, both women and men are able to identify meaningfully with the whole human race rather than only with their gender group, and this identification with the whole can dilute some of the dysfunctional intensities that necessarily flow from overly narrow gender identities (Hall, 1990b). The patterns of identification vary among different races, ethnic groups, and cultures, although consciousness must necessarily remain consistently related to all kinds of politics of empowerment (Collins, 1990).

RELIGIOUS DICTATES AND GENDER

Traditional western religions essentially dictate that human beings are either women or men and nothing in between (Erickson, 1993). This is particularly true, historically and in the present, of fundamentalism (Bendroth, 1994). Thus many religions emphasize and polarize sex differences, as well as spell out gender-based ethical responsibilities to procreate (Hussain, 1984). However, critically assessing the extent to which religions reflect nature or civilization serves to protect individuals and groups from their strongest distorting influences (Appleyard, 1993; Eisler, 1987). A questioning posture strengthens critical faculties and increases objectivity about the effects of religious influences on perceived and actual gender differences (Ryan, 1992). Comparisons of religious and ethical principles, for example, need to be related to gender socialization processes, and what it is said to take to be "more of a woman" or "more of a man" (Stoltenberg, 1989).

Although religious dictates can fulfill personal interests and develop individual potentials, they perhaps more frequently control and limit women (Daly, 1968) and sometimes men (Stoltenberg, 1989). However, following selected religious dictates can also create ways to develop spirituality. For example, increasing autonomy through strengthening spirituality enables people to become freer from conventional gender prescriptions, especially when political connections are recognized, as in feminist spirituality (Spretnak, 1982).

The fact that dichotomized gender models are so deeply embedded in major world religions and religious sects is evidence that sex is a primary basis for the organization of social institutions and society. Early preliterate societies, for example, were organized only along lines of sex and age. Past and present male stereotypes are pernicious influences in distorting human nature and social justice, as are past and present female stereotypes (Stoltenberg, 1989). But, even though throughout evolution women have been largely subordinated by men, religions and spirituality can provide ways for them to realize their authentic uniqueness and possibilities for collective action (Chopp, 1989; Erickson, 1993; Haney, 1989).

Because religious dictates are first experienced as being external to the self, they can be critically evaluated and selectively internalized rather than automatically absorbed. For example, people can become aware of differences between their parents' beliefs and their own understanding of religion. Identity thrives more through cumulative individual value choices than through passive acceptance of others' beliefs. The capacity to select constructive values must be strengthened for individuals to develop their human potential. When both women and men cultivate autonomy, they can create and sustain more meaningful identities in all aspects of their everyday interactions (Hall, 1990b).

GENDER AND THE CONCEPT OF GOD

People endow the object of their worship with supreme power and inestimable value. For example, Western religious beliefs are based on a concept of an omnipotent God. Where traditions are male-dominated, and male values are predominant and pervasive throughout society, the godheads of mainstream religions predictably reflect maleness, as in the United States. Similarly, where customs are feminine in style and substance, and female values are preeminent and pervasive, godheads predictably reflect femaleness. Taoism, for example, is a religion that endows female values with sacredness. When women and men are socially stratified, female and male values become stratified as well, and the value system of the dominant sex is worshipped or lauded more than that of the subordinated sex, as in ancient Rome. The resulting supremacy of one set of values necessarily means that other values are diminished and even trivialized. These patterns of values may not remain stable, however, and shifts have been documented over lengthy periods of time (Eisler, 1987).

Deepening one's understanding of the concept of God, and getting beyond arbitrary gender assignations, reduces bias and distortion in everyday negotiations. For example, if God is believed to be omnipotent, God must be both sexes as well as both genders, and at the same time be more than both. By definition, an all-powerful God cannot be anthropomorphic, so God must transcend whatever is associated with either sex and gender.

Nevertheless, it is characteristically human to see human images in the unknown, particularly where there are strong fears and desires (James, 1969). As a result of this understandable and perhaps necessary confusion, concepts of godheads may easily be merged with basic, if distorted, beliefs or stereotypes about masculinity and femininity, as in Hinduism. Sexual polarities are fundamental dichotomies of thought and organization that are crucial to human reflection (Chopp, 1989; Eisler, 1987). However, because concepts of God are polluted when limited notions of gender dominate thinking and religious experiences, perfectionist or utopian visions become essential for inspiring effective struggles for justice (Haney, 1989).

If gender is a primary source of patterns of worship—as in fertility religions or in societies that glorify war—rather than a belief in an all-powerful, neutral supreme being, people necessarily act only in their own self-interest, or in opposition to their self-interest. Ideally, the object of worship should be a just and omniscient God that transcends and thereby neutralizes all dichotomies of sex and gender. Meaningful contact and effective communication with such a supreme deity cannot be established through worship that is limited by gender concerns.

GENDER AND RELIGIOUS DEVOTIONS

In civilized societies, religious organizations and other complex groups tend to be hierarchical, as is, for example, the Roman Catholic church. Historical data also show that past and present industrialized and less developed societies are generally patriarchal (Lerner, 1986). Thus, in most societies, positions of power and leadership continue to be held by men rather than women (Ryan, 1992). Therefore, because of the nature of traditional social processes and forms, men successfully claim most leadership positions in religious organizations in modern societies, as well as in other social organizations (Ebaugh, 1993; Spretnak, 1982).

In many religious groups led by men, followers or subordinates may be men and women, or even solely women. This is particularly true in orthodox Judaism. Followers or subordinates are frequently overwhelmingly female where the power wielded by women is negligible compared with that wielded by men (Ryan, 1992). As a consequence, women become a relatively silent or passive majority, and religion has a silencing impact in women's socialization (Erickson, 1993).

In most religious organizations and communities, men usually lead and women usually follow. These trends are apparent throughout the United States and Western Europe. Men typically lead community prayers, give religious sacraments, and perform other kinds of religious rites, whereas women tend to be more involved in worship and devotional practices. To the extent that religious practices and religious experiences are subject to male dominance, women compose the lower echelons of religious organizations and participate in the relatively passive activities of practicing devotions and other minor religious rituals (Daly, 1968). This imbalance in women's and men's patterns of worship is particularly evident in highly traditional worldwide denominations such as Islam (Hussain, 1984).

However, if the goal of women's religious devotions is to make contact with supernatural powers or a godhead, prayer and meditation can reveal ways to overcome gender prohibitions (Haney, 1989). Thus women's customary devotions can be liberating, rather than merely ritualistic expressions of social status and the related belief systems (Chopp, 1989; Hall, 1990b). In this way, religious devotions may signal ways out of women's restricted life chances, and religions may inspire political activism (Lorentzen, 1991).

GENDER, RELIGIOUS BELIEFS, AND RELIGIOUS PRACTICES

Some of the most difficult tangles to unsnarl are the complexities inherent in relationships between gender and religions. Sometimes it is difficult to discern where religions begin and end, and where the impact of gender differences is (Eisler, 1987). Sometimes it seems that religious beliefs cannot be expressed without resorting to meanings derived from genders, nor religious practices performed without incorporating rituals, conventional statuses, and expectations related to gender (Chopp, 1989).

At least hypothetically, it is possible to have neutral supernatural powers or godheads, as well as to make commitments to religious beliefs that transcend personal characteristics and attributes of sex and gender (Spretnak, 1982). If humans could live outside the confines of gender roles, gender need not bias or restrict religious beliefs and practices (Haney, 1989). Even though most societies, in most times and in most places, have been organized around sexual stratification and male dominance through varied social forms and practices, sexual stratification within religions is not inevitable (Lerner, 1986). Therefore, even though gender, religious beliefs, and religious practices are inextricably related, their influences can be somewhat separated and understood and to some extent even neutralized (Hall, 1990b).

As has already been noted, the earliest communities were organized on sexual and age-related bases; these preliterate social forms were later expressed in specific religious beliefs and practices. The evolutionary and historical depth of the origins of sexual division of labor make it extremely difficult for religions to be free of gender overtones (Eisler, 1987). Religious beliefs and practices are thought of as the essence of religion (Durkheim, 1915), and gender concerns frequently remain at the core of these beliefs and practices (Bendroth, 1994; Hussain, 1984). However, cultivating and strengthening individual identities can provide ways out of the inhibiting overlaps among gender, religious beliefs, and religious practices. Selecting values with which to identify as individuals and groups can open up religious systems that are otherwise bound tightly by gender role expectations and gender stratification needs (Hall, 1990b).

RELIGIOUS SANCTIONS AND GENDER ROLES

The power of religions is frequently felt primarily through religious sanctions, which may virtually coerce individuals to behave in certain ways if they want to keep particular religious faiths and continue to exercise privileges of membership in them. This situation was particularly prevalent in Europe from the Middle Ages until the onset of the industrial revolution. Furthermore, it is primarily religious sanctions that polarize religious belief systems and their values into categories of right and wrong or good and evil, in efforts to clarify distinctions between the sacred and the profane. Ostracism and excommunication, for example, are real threats to remaining socially viable in many communities.

One of the ways in which religions control everyday activities is by extending their sanctions to sex, gender roles, and gender expectations. People are who they are, including their genders, largely because of ways in which particular kinds of behavior, such as sex relations, have been sacralized or demonized. Thus, gender choices are not free, and religions are primary sources of many sanctions that control sexual and gender behavior (Daly, 1968). The grip of narrow, gender-specific religious sanctions needs to be loosened to benefit the whole of society, and people should not have to pay the price of not belonging to a particular religion, or any religion, to free themselves from these negative influences (Haney, 1989). Thus, religious beliefs and practices must be modified for women and men to gain autonomy and strengthened identities, which can effectively neutralize some of the negative consequences of sacralized and demonized gender roles (Hall, 1990b).

Becoming more objective about oneself and one's cherished values brings detachment from conventional gender role prescriptions and expectations. Understanding how religious socialization—or possibly a lack of religious socialization—has resulted in honoring certain beliefs and values loosens their hold over the self. Most people initially absorb specific religious tenets uncritically, unless they have been expressly encouraged to be independent from an early age and therefore select their own values more freely. In these complex processes, religious sanctions run as deep as the religious beliefs and practices that sustain religions, and only when the basic tenets of religions themselves—such as obedience to the Pope in Roman Catholicism—are effectively questioned will the restrictive influences of religious sanctions be neutralized.

GENDER, SOCIAL CLASS, AND RELIGION

Gender is a fundamental basis for social stratification systems in both preliterate and civilized societies (Lerner, 1986). Gender expectations accompanying sexual divisions of labor are deep-seated influences on all forms of social stratification and are very difficult to modify or neutralize. Social mobility occurs when individuals create visions of circumstances that go beyond their present empirical conditions and act on those visions, thereby making new situations possible (Haney, 1989). To progress toward realizing the goals of change related to such visions, however, individuals must have sufficient motivation to sustain action in this direction (Ryan, 1992). For example, individuals who believe their work results from a religious vocation, or is dictated by God's will, tend to be extremely conscientious and productive.

Hope for a freer future rests on individuals being able to transcend social class restrictions, which include gender stratification (Eisler, 1987). Sometimes this work includes activism and being involved in social movement ideologies; both secular and religious belief systems can be instrumental in bringing about substantial social change (Ryan, 1992). Although many women and men are impeded by religious gender stereotypes, some religious or moral values can help to transform limitations by becoming motivators to promote change (Hall, 1991). Religious motivation is also sustained through long periods of time, because it is made up of atemporal sacred forces and influences. For example, doing God's will in Judeo-Christian traditions may be a sustained, powerful motivator for both women and men who want to make long-term egalitarian changes in their social relations.

GENDER, IDENTITY, AND RELIGION

Giving attention to strengthening individual identity may go so far as to neutralize individual and social influences of gender and religion. Such consequences occur because identity reflects the most autonomous part of the self, which selects and nurtures chosen values, and people act from these deeply held values.

Identity challenges people to be selective about both their gender values and their religious values. Concentrating on uniqueness and on accomplishing specific goals focuses individual behavior, with the result that conventional programming for gender and religious values can be withstood more meaningfully and more effectively. Thus, identity empowerment is a means to freedom; strengthening identity increases detachment and objectivity about many different kinds of choices. With strengthened identities, people no longer reactively conform to others' expectations or wishes, but rather follow their own internal promptings. In contrast to gender and religions, which frequently exert pressures toward conformity to social stereotypes, identity is based on uniqueness and deliberately chosen ideals, which generate people's most important goals and objectives. Identity encourages people to be innovative and creative, rather than to act out roles that reinforce traditional goals, ultimately challenging or changing rather than sustaining established social structures.

Thus identity is a significant mechanism through which people can transcend conventional gender and religious stereotypes. Frequently, however, it is through communing with supernatural powers that people are enabled to define and express their true identities. From a Judeo-Christian point of view, creating and acting from one's own identity can also be thought of as living in grace, or doing God's will. In this respect, religious and secular vocations are essentially discoveries and revelations of identities through prayer, meditation, or everyday behavior.

A strong identity neutralizes or wards off some of the restrictive influences of gender and religion, and can be understood as increasing immunity to dysfunctions. Identity empowerment also reduces the symbiosis that otherwise exists between gender stereotypes and conservative religious influences. Clinically speaking, identity is a way out of behavioral restrictions of sexual stereotypes, as well as a kind of salvation from the overly narrow religious rituals of conventional devotions (Haney, 1989).

QUESTIONS AND ANSWERS

Two significant questions related to identity and religion are: "Is a life of the spirit truly available for all?" and "Does gender make it more difficult for women than men to have access to supernatural powers?" Two related questions are: "Why, and in which ways, are social expectations for women and men so different that men, more easily than women, consistently achieve powerful positions within religions as well as in society?" and "Why do women have lower status than men within religions, being more content to busy themselves with devotional religious practices than to pursue leadership within religious communities?"

One answer to these varied concerns is that sexism is so pervasive, and so deeply institutionalized, that it is present in all social settings. Furthermore, not only are women discriminated against, but they also limit their own opportunities through internalizing specific traditional values and conventional beliefs about women. However, a woman's place is not necessarily in the home, and women need not be mothers to gain others' respect. Even though widespread patterns of women's subordination have been substantiated empirically, it does not follow that they are predetermined or inevitable. If future conditions promote increased freedom and autonomy for women, it is conceivable that women will assume correspondingly more powerful roles in religious organizations, as well as be recognized as having as much access to supernatural powers as men.

Additional concerns about Western religions are reflected in questions such as: "Is it necessary for God to be represented as a male figure who is considered to be a father?" and "Is God's will different for women and for men?" and "Can religion free women from restricted conditions like subordination, stereotypes, and passivity?" Although it is difficult to reverse, or even modify, patriarchal traditions that are associated with the concept of God in Western civilizations, this notion of a supreme power is so much more than a male authority that any reduction to gender terms diminishes much of the richness of religious experiences, spiritual communion, and worship. Ideally, God's will is spiritually "equal" for women and men, and at best religions can serve to free women from subordination, stereotypes, and passivity.

GENERALIZATIONS

Gender stereotypes are generally reinforced more in religions than in spirituality. In fact, although frequently in veiled terms, the doctrinal beliefs of traditional Western religions usually label male values as "good," and female values as "evil." Furthermore, the godhead in Western civilization is fairly consistently referred to as "He" or "Father."

These facts set up an emotional tone in many religions that suggests it is more advantageous to be male than female in our culture because being male is associated with being good, being superior, and having power. By contrast, female values are associated with being evil, being passive, and being subordinate. These influences result in rather dramatic polarizations of males and females, as well as in women's disempowerment (Eisler, 1987).

Religious values associated with gender distinctions are intensely emotion-laden and reinforce the cultural and traditional polarities that already exist between women and men (Hussain, 1984). However, some degree of social mobility becomes possible through changing women's motivations. For example, specific religious values can inspire individual women to challenge cultural stereotypes, as well as to create visions of more egalitarian communities.

Gender roles tend to be either sacralized or demonized through positive and negative religious sanctions (Daly, 1968). Religions frequently endorse double moral standards for women and men, which, because expectations for women are more demanding, are difficult for women to keep. However, the more aware women are of the many controls religious sanctions exert, the freer they are to create alternatives to those expectations. For example, when women are able to reverse some of the effects of negative religious sanctions, they can confront and neutralize male authorities more effectively in both religious and social contexts. Even though, historically, women's subordination has persisted through long periods of time, there have been occasional breakthroughs, and it is now more widely recognized that the past need not determine the future (Erickson, 1993).

PROPOSITIONS

Strengthening women's individual and group identities can modify women's subordination, in spite of the strong reinforcement of such subordination by religious sanctions. The more women strengthen their identities through internalizing constructive values, the more they can neutralize or at least diminish their subordination.

Women can also gain more equal access to supernatural powers by reversing some of their socialization, and by changing their responses to the negative religious sanctions that largely define and restrict their gender roles (Chopp, 1989). In a male-dominated patriarchy, women and men can usefully be thought of as members of two distinct social classes, with women belonging to a social class that has lower status than the class of men. However, because avenues of social mobility exist for both women and men, their respective status positions may shift to the extent that women make different value choices.

Although a life of the spirit may be hypothetically available for everyone, women generally have to overcome barriers created by gender socialization as a prerequisite for their own spiritual advancement (Haney, 1989). Blocks to women's progress are removed or decreased by selecting individual and group values that increase women's mobility. The process of barrier reduction also neutralizes the effects of gender stereotypes, so that women's and men's expectations become less polarized and distorted (Stoltenberg, 19889).

Religions generally reinforce social processes by both positively and negatively sanctioning behavior, which is acceptable or unacceptable according to conventional gender norms and standards. However, the power of these sanctions decreases to the extent that individuals are able to reverse or neutralize the religious pressures to conform. Some degree of deliberate choice is necessary to accomplish a decrease in the impact of religious sanctions, because reactive or automatic behavior predictably follows lines of least resistance by accommodating to strong religious or social influences (Cornwall, 1987).

CHOICES

Although gender distinctions are usually based on biological sexual differences, relationships between sex and gender are indirect rather than direct, causal, or deterministic. In other words, patterns in gender behavior result from individual and social choices, whereas biological sexual differences are ascribed and involuntary.

The fact that gender results from choices has important consequences. This reality means that it is possible to change gender choices, so that distorting or restrictive gender stereotypes are modified or even eradicated. By inference, people are able to influence gender patterns and their reinforcements if they make deliberate, concerted efforts to choose values that increase freedom for all.

To some extent people create their own destinies as they choose ways in which to be women or men, ways in which to be religious or spiritual, and ways in which to be themselves. Choice is a vital component of freedom, survival, and fulfillment, especially when contradictions among families, gender, religion, and identity need to be resolved.

One major choice is to move away from stereotyped expectations in religious experiences, gender roles, and gender responsibilities. Having realistic views is advantageous for making changes, and denying facts or reacting to others' pressures limits opportunities. Autonomy and distinctiveness must be maintained for individuals to make the myriad choices necessary for defining gender and beliefs. When reality and talents are demystified, actions become more effective (Gerth & Mills, 1953).

Gender differences as well as the stereotypes associated with gender are explored in the case that follows.

CASE STUDY

Sophie Maynard was a 35-year-old, White, Roman Catholic woman, married, with four young children. Sophie went to church regularly and prayed several times a day in her private devotions. By contrast, Sophie's husband, although also a Roman Catholic, spent very little time observing or thinking about religion. He had not attended church regularly for many years.

Sophie had a stressful marriage, but did not want to resort to divorce because it would violate her religious convictions. She sought counseling to help her to adjust to this painful situation, and even to allow her to think the impossible thought of divorcing her husband.

Sophie was also pressured by her in-laws, who thought that if she pleased her husband better she could reduce the frictions in her marriage. Because her in-laws had given her family gifts of money in the past, Sophie felt dependent on them and accepted their view that her marital problems are somehow related to her lack of interest in her husband.

Through a course of therapy that lasted for 6 months, Sophie was able to focus more effectively on her own responsibilities, and at the same time she began to worry less about what her husband and in-laws thought of her. This clearing of her confusion allowed Sophie to decide what it is she wanted to do with her life, regardless of her marital status.

Clinical sessions helped Sophie to manage conflict with her husband and strengthened her capacity to cope with her in-laws. Furthermore, by managing her time and energy more effectively, Sophie was able to plan a career for herself. Because she already had a degree in psychology, she applied for a position as a school counselor, a job which would give her school holiday time with her own children.

As Sophie continued to attend church and pray throughout the course of her therapy, she began to see that she had alternatives to conforming to the expectations of her husband and in-laws. Although all these significant others resisted her newfound independence—for example, her husband tried to prevent her from assuming work responsibilities out of the home—Sophie was able to move ahead with her plans in spite of the conflict. Thus Sophie's understanding of the broader picture of her life inspired her to make significant changes, which ultimately lowered the tensions in her relationship with her husband.

Analysis

Clinical strategies included encouraging Sophie to reevaluate her dependency on her husband. Through the course of therapy she strengthened her identity sufficiently to be able to reduce this dependency, and this change then allowed her to move more freely toward a career of her choice.

Sophie's new centering of her life on her own needs improved the ways in which she coped with demands from her children and in-laws. For example, with the help of her therapist, she increased her awareness of the decisions she made on a daily basis, enabling herself to use her time and energy more efficiently.

Sophie used her religious faith to support her often difficult-to-accomplish changes, and she continued to develop her spirituality and spiritual resources through family confrontations. She also used her psychological know-how to strengthen her professional contributions to the school system, and to make sure that her value choices were consistent with her goals and concerns for family survival and well-being. She no longer experienced her Roman Catholic beliefs as requiring strict obedience to family conventions, but rather as providing world views for helping her to see the broader picture of her life.

Sophie was able to live more comfortably with the religious differences between herself and her husband, and she no longer felt the urge to be the religious director of her family. This kind of gender expectation had severely limited her freedom and creativity in the past. Sophie also learned how to live more comfortably with other kinds of differences between her husband and herself, thereby seeing herself as a person who counted on her own, rather than merely her husband's helper.

After 6 months of therapy Sophie was able to visualize yet another career change for herself once she had spent a year or more as a school counselor. She began to understand that her supportive professional role as a counselor was similar to her roles as wife and mother, and she became interested in pursuing a career in higher education in the long run. Because Sophie had a strong interest in teaching and research methodologies, she decided that when her children were older, she would like to complete a doctorate in education. Her therapist encouraged her to formulate this dream more clearly and to keep it alive by considering what she needed to do to move in this professional direction.

STRATEGIES FOR CLINICAL INTERVENTIONS

The success of clinical interventions depends largely on the quality or depth of demystification that occurs through clinical exchanges. Because gender is one of the most powerful socializing influences, to understand how religions and identities interact and affect each other, the impact of gender values on these processes must be examined. Furthermore, because gender, religion, and family interaction are all compelling factors in individual and group experiences, they need to be scrutinized and neutralized if possible whenever clinical discussions focus on clients' everyday decision making.

Although gender influences in clinical progress are not yet sufficiently documented (Erickson, 1993), other kinds of research on gender highlight clinical issues (Collins, 1990; Stoltenberg, 1989). This knowledge is particularly important in strengthening efforts to assess the influences of gender, identity, and religions in daily behavior and therapy (Chopp, 1989; Hall, 1990b; Randour, 1993).

Another stage in a demystification of gender influences in interaction is clinicians' active fostering of clients' critical faculties through encouraging clients to question the assumptions they make about reality (Glassner & Freedman, 1979). Clinicians have many opportunities to invite clients to question the sources of the values they express, as well as merely to ask clients questions about their functioning (Randour, 1993). Objectivity and criticism sharpen clients' awareness about the influence of gender on identity and religion issues.

As well as demystifying clients' views of the self and the universe through clinical interventions, optimally clinicians ask clients to define themselves and become increasingly authentic in expressing their genders, religions, and personal uniqueness (Pollner, 1989). Furthermore, clinicians increase their personal and professional effectiveness when they understand their own functioning positions in relation to the influences of gender, religion, and individuality. In fact, it is only when this kind of awareness has been attained that clinicians can assist their clients to see the broader pictures of their lives with respect to gender, religion, and personal uniqueness most effectively.

Clinicians understand the depth of gender influences more fully when they relate specific behavior and gender standards to family dynamics. Clinicians' continued efforts to examine clients' behavior and preferences in the broadest contexts of their lives allows clinicians to recognize and deal with clients as whole persons. Microscopic or more limited bases of clinical analyses are necessarily correspondingly limited in their usefulness. Clinical data suggest that clinicians are both more responsible and have more constructive professional results when they broaden their theoretical perspectives to account for the impact of genders on identity and religion (Erickson, 1993).

10 Clinical Tasks

1. Assess the extent to which clients are consciously self-identified as women and men.
2. Determine which views or values of the clients have the strongest influence on their gender definitions.
3. Discuss how clients' behavior is blocked by beliefs in sexual stereotypes.
4. Examine how clients may be released from the power of sexual stereotypes.
5. Link clients' views of gender to their family dependencies and social experiences.
6. Heighten clients' awareness about links between their beliefs about gender and their religious beliefs.
7. Discuss clients' religious activities in relation to their views of gender.
8. Describe ways to separate religious and gender socialization processes in examining sex roles and responsibilities.
9. Link clients' views of interpersonal gender issues to broad social and political trends in gender relations and feminism.
10. Encourage clients to define their own personal and social goals in relation to societal sexual stereotypes and sex role expectations.

Chapter 7

Social Class and Religion

All too often the existence of direct associations between social class membership and religious affiliation is publicly denied, especially in the United States where equal opportunity and individualism are essential components of national ideologies (Finke & Stark, 1992; Kosmin & Lachman, 1993). Furthermore, public opinion mistakenly cherishes the idea that religions are pure and untainted by social concerns, and derive from divine sources. For example, young children are taught religious "truths" rather than the history or social contexts of religious belief systems. However, from both evolutionary and historical perspectives religions have been viewed, described, and explained as social products (Ashbrook, 1993; Finke & Stark, 1992; Smith, 1991). Furthermore, people can become freer of the effects of social class biases in religion if they understand at least some ways in which social classes and religions influence each other (Cornwall, 1987).

Religions and social classes interact in complex change processes that can to some extent be delineated within the environmental and social contexts of evolution, and the history of oppression and industrialization (Herberg, 1955). On a more personal basis, religion can both reinforce social status and be an inspiration or source of motivation for social mobility (Goode, 1968).

When deliberately making moves to strengthen their identities, individuals make value choices to define how they may or may not be involved in social classes and religions (Hall, 1990a). Individuals and religions may emphasize the spiritual aspects of communion between individuals and supernatural powers in an effort to transcend the influences of social classes (Randour, 1993). In this way sufficient motivation to overcome or neutralize social class influences can be acquired, especially because, for example, doing God's will and living in grace are not usually synonymous with following social class trends and lifestyles. People also become more autonomous and independent when they identify with values that are not directly tied to social status (Roof, 1992).

Like social class in that it is ascribed at birth, religious affiliation frequently becomes an extension of social status. Denominational religions such as Protestantism, Roman Catholicism, and Judaism can be understood in terms of cultural heritage and social mobility, as well as in terms of their specific belief systems. It is meaningful for individuals to scrutinize the social origins of their religious beliefs, because this knowledge will eventually increase their autonomy, whether they accept or reject their families' religious traditions. A broad analysis puts historical and political sources of religious beliefs into better perspective than is possible through examining currents of popular opinion (Berger & Luckmann, 1967; Lerner, 1986).

RELIGION AND EVOLUTION

Religions usually incorporate explanations of the earliest phases of physical and human evolution into their histories or doctrines (Hess, 1991). Religions are significant participants in evolution, and they have been and are sometimes still regarded as sources of knowledge or "the truth" about the creation of the universe (Lenski, 1961). Religions provided essentially the first social theories about how society came into being, and of the nature of humanity (Berger & Luckmann, 1967; Durkheim, 1915).

Religions define experiences as good or evil; and this dualism provides a primitive basic division of thought into cause and effect (Durkheim, 1915). Whereas religions tend to reinforce dualistic thinking, spirituality and different forms of mysticism go beyond such dichotomies (Randour, 1993). Spirituality is essentially a synthesis of beliefs and experiences that emerges at a later stage of evolution of consciousness, when individuals can be less dependent on their primary groups for survival and fulfillment (Haught, 1984; McNamara, 1992; Mol, 1978). Both a heightened individual awareness and an increased social awareness make spirituality possible (Haney, 1989).

To a certain extent, religions anchor complex evolutionary processes in human meanings such as values and ideals (Weber, 1958). People get a sense of being part of their own creation and evolution through the value choices they make, especially their most cherished values, which inevitably make up their identities (Hall, 1986b). Religions orient individuals to the world and to the universe, as well as give meanings for seeing and thinking about themselves as participants in evolution (Strunk, 1979). Religions may also either increase the oppression of lower social classes or, conversely, increase social mobility in industrialized societies (Weber, 1958). Thus social classes can be reinforced, modified, or transformed through religious beliefs and motivations (Beckford & Luckmann, 1989; Hammond, 1992).

Social classes are integral parts of evolution in that they represent relatively advanced stages of human social development. In the earliest societies, most social stratification was rigid, and was based on sex and age differences (Eisler, 1987). Later, more complex class systems emerged, frequently based on economic resources as well as on religions, races, ethnicity, and sexual orientation (Ryan, 1992). In such contexts, religions frequently reinforce social class circumstances in that they make up the value bases of people's everyday realities (Berger & Luckmann, 1967).

To the extent that religions support social stratification and keep existing social classes in place, religions impede evolution. For example, rigid class lifestyles can limit educational and technical progress, as in the north of England. However, whenever religions or religious beliefs become an impetus for social change, they expedite historical and evolutionary processes, as in the United States. Thus religions not only can restrict people to their social classes, but also can support individuals and groups who want to shift their statuses. Religions can provide people with purpose and direction in their individual everyday lives, adding a sense of progress to their understanding of impersonal evolutionary changes. Some evolutionary changes may be thought of as increased elevations in consciousness, as well as increases in the size of the human brain (Ashbrook, 1993; Teilhard de Chardin, 1965). Religions try to make sense out of what might otherwise be uncomfortable experiences of chaos or meaninglessness (Jung, 1933).

At the same time that religions honor the status quo of social class systems, they can call into question many of the assumptions made about those same social classes; and recognizing contradictions between religions and social realities increases public criticism. It is sometimes difficult to reconcile religious and secular beliefs, especially where they relate to equality and inequality. In fact, the special interests of social classes have meant so much historically that people have been willing to lose their lives both to sustain and to eradicate these differences (Eisler, 1987; Lerner, 1986). Furthermore, some people essentially sell their souls to live according to others' ideals (Appleyard, 1993; Hess, 1991).

RELIGION AND OPPRESSION

To the extent that religions express social class affiliations, such as Baptist sects in the United States, religions are also intimately associated with relationships between different social classes. In addition to being status symbols and reference groups, religions describe and protect specific world views. When religions represent wealthy, dominant social classes, as in the Episcopalian denomination, they necessarily contribute to the exploitation of members of less privileged social classes through their support of the status quo. By contrast, when religions represent the interests of minority groups or classes of people who have few assets, as small Protestant sects tend to do, they may promote social change, even revolution (Lorentzen, 1991).

Religions affect the secular powers of their believers either by giving attention to social realities or by diverting attention away from immediate living conditions. Religions can actively promote social activism, or activism may progress in spite of the conservative influences of religion (Ryan, 1992). When religious beliefs are associated with worldly success, attention becomes more focused on distributions of income and other assets (Weber, 1958). However, by contrast, if religions are directed toward working for salvation, or life after death, hazardous living conditions may be ignored or denied (Marty & Appleby, 1991). Thus religions either heighten consciousness about possibilities for change or magnify devotional practices so much that practical strategies for improving living conditions cannot be formulated. When religions obfuscate social realities they automatically increase the oppression of lower social classes and reinforce the interests of upper social classes. To the extent that religions increase inequality rather than expedite human progress toward equality, faith in just supernatural powers is necessarily contradicted (Pollner, 1989). However, individuals can neutralize some of the negative effects of religion by focusing on enhancing identity through selecting meaningful religious values, at the same time responsibly ensuring that these values will work toward freeing increased numbers of people in society (Hall, 1991).

RELIGION AND INDUSTRIALIZATION

As makers of social change, the belief systems and perspectives of some religions have supported increased industrialization during the past 300 years (Weber, 1958). For example, by emphasizing individual initiative and hard work, Protestantism influenced the early stages of the industrial revolution in Europe. Similarly, in Asia, Shintoism and other religions have been associated with industrialization, and Buddhism and Hinduism with a lack of industrialization (Yinger, 1957).

These correlations suggest that religions are more than background factors in intercultural differences, and that beliefs and values play crucial roles in establishing both work styles and lifestyles, as in the case of Shintoism in Japan. Commitments of time and energy are influenced by particular beliefs and depend on the world views and assumptions about human nature implied by those beliefs. This is particularly evident in religions that provide extreme contrasts with Western religions, such as in Hinduism. Whatever is defined as sacred is especially important; these values will make up individuals' and groups' most cherished ideals.

To the extent that societies pursue industrialization and secularism, the quality of religious beliefs may change. For example, becoming worldly and materialistic can lead to getting involved in secular concerns about communities and societies in ways that were not possible before improved communications. Modern technology makes the world a smaller place for many people, and mass secular education has opened up new universes for members of more social classes. One consequence of such changes is that access to supernatural powers appears to be increasingly dependent on personal efforts, and life chances do not seem to depend as much on divine intervention (Hammond, 1992). Decisions flow from these kinds of changes in assumptions, and people necessarily define themselves and their potentials differently today from the way they did in earlier historical periods (James, 1969). However, as societies become more complex, character and value choices result increasingly from particular social structures, and basic social institutions have significant consequences for individual and social behavior (Gerth & Mills, 1953).

RELIGION AND SOCIAL STATUS

Religions have their own social statuses within society, which automatically transfer to members of their congregations. These social factors may also influence religious beliefs and commitments (Cornwall, 1987). In general, denominations such as Protestantism tend to have higher social statuses than sects, in that they have already been institutionalized to some extent and are integral parts of mainstream society (Lenski, 1961). On the other hand, the social statuses of sects are relatively low, because sects have peripheral locations in society. Therefore sects frequently have lower social prestige than denominations (Herberg, 1955).

Although people usually do not become members of a particular religion to attain a specific social status, changing religions can be an effective means of achieving a higher status (Lenski, 1961). People cannot escape some of the labelling consequences of being members of particular religions, but being born into a religion merely ascribes status. To the extent that an individual actively achieves status, he or she may decide to change ascribed religious status at any time.

Facts that show how religions are closely tied to social statuses challenge beliefs that religion is solely the worship of godheads. In this respect, what was historically believed to be the essence of religion is polluted. Furthermore, different religious affiliations are also characterized by varied social class styles (Goode, 1968). Whereas denominations accommodate and adapt to societal goals and social needs, which are best described as mundane rather than transcendental, spirituality is generally characterized by yearnings for deeper mystical experiences. Unlike religion, spirituality is one of human beings' more successful attempts to stay united and in communion with supernatural powers or a godhead, at the same time having relative disregard for earthly references and standards (Randour, 1993).

Therefore, although religions may be influential in defining social statuses, such definitions are not fixed and can be changed by changing religions or by changing ways in which a particular religion is expressed—for example, by moving from a denomination to a sect or from a sect to a denomination. Because links between religions and social statuses are dynamic rather than static, these relationships can be modified under most circumstances.

RELIGION AND SOCIAL MOBILITY

Switching religions is a tried and true avenue for social mobility (Lenski, 1961). For example, moving from a lower-status religion to a higher automatically raises social status. In this way most religions at least partially define opportunities for mobility and elevated social status.

A less crude, and perhaps more effective, way of increasing social mobility in the long run, however, is to increase motivation to achieve particular secular goals, such as professional development, through increasing the intensity of certain religious beliefs, or incorporating specific religious values in everyday activities. When people really believe that it is morally right for them to move in particular directions, achievements increase, and the statuses or responsibilities they aspire to will more likely be attained.

Religions frequently reinforce social class membership, whereas, by contrast, spirituality tends to increase individual efforts to transcend social class. Social mobility results from strengthening identities, and strengthened identities result from value choices grounded in religions. Thus social mobility is a way to get out of the limiting conditions endemic to specific social classes, and religion is a vehicle to enhance social mobility.

Religions are significant influences in social mobility, because they provide meaning, purpose, direction, and motivation for attaining higher levels of functioning. Religions sacralize the ordinary, including explanations about receiving either religious or secular vocations, and they add emotional tones and valences to everyday routines. These effects may inspire changes in the status quo of society, as well as in particular positions within society. To a large extent, the highest individual and social achievements depend on deciding both who to be and what to do. Religions strengthen moral purpose and provide a sense of having specific objectives to be achieved. In these ways, religions magnify and illuminate moral choices and social options. For example, the whole picture of society, as well as individual characters and personalities, is seen more clearly through a particular religion, such as Islam. Religions are powerful moral and social forces that can propel and advance individuals and groups out of their current statuses.

IDENTITY AND RELIGION

Identity is a catalyst that changes relationships between social classes and religions. When religious beliefs are examined and seen for what they are in the context of social class memberships, people are more able to select their own values, such as political involvement. Value choices modify religious influences on both individual and collective behavior, including institutional processes between social classes and religions.

Identities may be empowered by religious values, such as truth and divine justice, which eventually bring about changes in class structures. Religious beliefs frequently provide sufficient motivation to carry through actions that create shifts in the statuses of individuals and groups, largely by giving meaning to everyday activities. Purpose and direction can be found in the mundane, and identities strengthened by religion enhance individual functioning.

A focus on identity shows ways in which religion has impeded people in the past, and has perhaps kept them in their social classes through sanctions and prescribed beliefs in the sacred. Identity issues also bring gender and family concerns into focus, which themselves influence correlations between social class and religion. Gender-specific analyses of life situations can help individuals clarify goals and objectives to be accomplished, which are then incorporated in identities as ideals and thereby realized in action.

SOCIAL CLASS AND RELIGION

All social classes are influenced by the pervasiveness of religion. Whether people are grouped according to age, sex, economic assets, education, race, ethnic group, or sexual orientation, they find that some religious beliefs and practices impinge on or expand their rights and responsibilities within and among classes. Links between social classes and religions are perceived as being so close that religions such as Roman Catholicism are perceived as solely restricting people to their class positions and inhibiting social change, especially social mobility. In this respect religions are thought of as being aligned with societal power and as depending on material assets as well as family procreation for their well-being and continuity.

Spirituality, like identity, cuts through close alliances between religions and established social classes, and anchors individuals in otherworldly values rather than social class values. When individual aspects of being rather than group memberships are emphasized, the dictates of class influences can be transcended. Spirituality allows for the recognition that individuals belong to the universal human race, rather than merely to particular social classes or interest groups within a society. This view motivates action from bases of different ideals and purposes. To be more free, it is necessary for individuals to break out of the restrictive interactions between religions and social classes, so that religions can give people a voice to combat their sense of powerlessness (Chopp, 1989).

From the perspective of history, religions and social classes remain inextricably related through time, whatever the social and political circumstances (Herberg, 1955). In fact, it is difficult—and sometimes impossible—for either spirituality or identity to loosen some of the tightly overlapping institutional influences. Although oppression and industrialization have varied the patterns of association between religions and social classes, individual social mobility continues to be difficult to achieve, especially in more traditional societies, such as India and many African countries. Even when secularism and modernity appear to expedite changes in status, these changes may be short-lived unless individuals are sufficiently resourceful to develop their own spiritualities and identities (Haney, 1989).

QUESTIONS AND ANSWERS

A haunting question that focuses on the central issues of identity and religion is "To what extent is religious experience a social class phenomenon?" Most people prefer to deny the existence of any correlation between religious affiliation and social class membership, in that this association reduces the prized sense that religions are, or should be, pure, and that religions have divine origins or supreme purposes rather than social sources and uses. However, evidence indicates that individuals frequently change religious communities as they become socially mobile, and furthermore that membership in religious denominations generally bestows higher social status than membership in religious sects.

Other related questions to be asked are "How do religions motivate individuals and groups to become socially mobile?" and "Do value choices merely define ways in which members of different social classes behave?" Because of the complexity of society, although religions may be sources of value choices, the purposes and directions received from these values usually go beyond particular social class lifestyles. In the long run, perhaps it is spirituality rather than religions that allows individuals to transcend social class and materialistic concerns, in that values from spiritual sources are necessarily less tied to worldly reference points than religious values. In any event, with respect to both religions and spirituality, concepts such as God's will have widespread applications, rather than narrowly defined associations with social classes.

Ultimately, identity and religion issues must also deal with the question "Do religions inevitably oppress members of lower social classes?" This question reflects the convictions and historical experiences of many different kinds of people, and it is difficult to shake off associations of religious beliefs with social, economic, and political privileges. However, individual interpretations of religious experiences can have significant constructive impacts on action, and religions do not oppress all members of lower social classes or other classes.

GENERALIZATIONS

Religious affiliation is an indicator of social class membership rather than a determinant of social class (Lenski, 1961). Religious observances make up part of a cluster of behaviors that distinguish social classes from each other without being definitive proof of specific class membership. Although religions frequently reinforce lifestyles associated with particular social classes, religions are much more than social class lifestyles.

Devotional practices of women and members of lower social classes tend to reinforce the status quo of society by keeping their practitioners in subordinate positions (Spretnak, 1982), because prayer, meditation, and reading sacred literature may not be forward-looking or directly related to secular living conditions. Paradoxically, however, some religious practices can serve as avenues of social mobility, as long as liberating and constructive religious values are emphasized in their adherents' regular observances and everyday behavior.

Spirituality, which historically is practiced by individuals rather than communities of believers, is less directly associated with social classes than are religions (Haney, 1989). Spirituality emphasizes inner religious experiences rather than rituals, and points more to mystical experiences and universal communion with godheads than to external behavior. Thus, spirituality is closer to what is generally considered to be pure religious observance, because it is relatively untainted by worldly concerns. Spirituality also encourages individuals' oneness with supernatural powers, or oneness with the universe, rather than mere acceptance by particular religious communities.

Religions either effectively extend social class cultures or lead toward social class changes. People break away from social class norms by developing a broader view of the universe and by allowing their new visions to be guides for individual and social fulfillment (Hess, 1991). In this respect religions provide releases from social class confines, as well as ways to go beyond social class categories.

PROPOSITIONS

The more individuals conform to specific religious practices, the more easily they can be thought of as belonging to a particular social class. For example, if religious practices are based on beliefs in a life to come, with a stronger emphasis on the hereafter than on present circumstances, there is a greater likelihood that these practices will limit achievements and lead to rejections of worldly success. Thus religions can generate restrictive influences on social attainments and contributions to society, and may appear—especially to outsiders—to oppress their believers by keeping them locked into their social statuses.

On the other hand, some kinds of religious beliefs motivate believers to break out of their social classes by becoming more socially mobile. Even though this situation may not promote extensive freedom, it frequently results in some shifting of social class allegiances. However, although religions may be means of changing social classes, in and of themselves they may not be able to release their believers from the need to conform to some kind of social class lifestyles (Goode, 1968).

By contrast, spirituality places a stronger emphasis on inner communion with a godhead than religions, and is therefore necessarily less directly related to social class experiences. The mystical, more universalist characteristics of spirituality promote broader visions of possibilities than religions, together with fewer this-world references and applications. When spirituality provides values for motivation, behavior related to these values is directed less toward social class achievements than toward improving religious experiences. Spirituality is thus more focused on acknowledging membership in the human race than membership in a particular social class.

In recent history, religions have motivated individuals and societies to meet many different needs in modern, industrialized societies (Appleyard, 1993). Religious world views are significant influences in societies' necessary adaptations to industrialization (Weber, 1958). Religions are therefore significant modes of social adjustment and have contributed to the growth of the middle classes during economic and industrial changes (Lenski, 1961).

CHOICES

One choice for individuals is to be influenced more strongly by spiritual beliefs or by social class affiliations. Even though this choice is not simple or clear-cut, and is infinitely more complex than such polarities suggest, behavior is in fact contingent on the priorities established in values and belief systems. Adherence to values that are primarily descriptive of social class interests is necessarily followed by conformity to corresponding mundane standards and ideals. By contrast, a greater concern for broad frames of reference derived from spirituality predictably promotes freer and more detached lifestyles than those dictated by social class interests.

To the extent that religious affiliation merely reflects social class membership, religion may not be liberating in its experiential consequences. By contrast, and as will be shown in the case study that follows, spirituality frequently promotes freedom to transcend social class values and ideals, because choosing to focus on union or a continuing close relationship with supernatural powers or a godhead reduces concerns about social class issues. Thus, choosing to ignore social class concerns strengthens orientation to spiritual values, and choosing spirituality frequently moves people out of their social class restrictions. Choosing to be committed to social class lifestyles ties people to specific expectations and roles. In fact, the choice to develop detailed social class refinements may require adherence to specific traditions, which then essentially causes a turning away from more inclusive goals and ideals. This kind of decision sets individual lives on specific courses for decades or more—which is why value choices need to be recognized as significant determinants of life outcomes.

CASE STUDY

Richard Morris was a 40-year-old single White man who lived in a suburb of Washington, DC. He had been professionally successful in a small business throughout his working life. However, as he approached middle age he felt that he had not accomplished enough for other people, and this distressed him a great deal. He was particularly aware that he had not married, had any children, or committed himself to any public interest or social issue.

Richard sought therapy to help him to find more meaning in his everyday life. He had lost touch with many of his family members over the years, and so he had become relatively isolated from his origins, even though most of his family members lived within 50 miles of his home. Richard had also rejected his family religion of Episcopalian Protestantism, and he had not attended church for about 20 years.

In the course of his therapy, which lasted for about a year, Richard began to discover how he might spend his time and energy in more worthwhile ways. Instead of aiming only for social mobility and an upper-class lifestyles, he decided to see how he could help children in his local community. He volunteered to be a mentor to young boys who had committed juvenile offenses, and he became involved in their school and personal lives.

Richard also decided to attend his local Methodist church. He enjoyed singing and he applied to be and was accepted as a member of the church choir. He found that his Methodist congregation was much more friendly and supportive than the Episcopal church he had attended as a boy, and he thrived from the supportive community contacts.

Richard made new friends through his church-going activities, and he also reestablished contact with his family. He soon felt himself to be more of a real person, and he was pleased to be expressing values different from those he had thought were required for professional achievement. As Richard's priorities changed, he was able to see himself and his preferences more clearly, and he planned to make other major changes related to his job in an effort to fit in more with his newfound lifestyle. His successes with mentoring gave him a sense of personal satisfaction that he had not been able to feel during his many years of professional work.

Analysis

Richard progressed well in clinical sessions because he was painfully restless and dissatisfied with his current life situation. He knew that he wanted to make some fairly drastic changes, but he needed guidance and a sense of direction to clarify his options and make satisfactory choices.

Richard benefitted a great deal from reestablishing contact with members of his family and from joining a Methodist congregation. The fact that he assumed an active role in this church community, as a member of the church choir, was particularly useful in meeting his need to be better integrated with local groups.

His new expressive forms of worship contrasted with his Episcopalian upbringing, and also served to free Richard from the restrictions he had felt in his middle-class lifestyle.

Richard reduced his felt isolation by establishing meaningful community and family contacts, and he allowed the Methodist religion to orient him toward otherworldly values that replaced his strived-for upper-class traditions. He began to believe that his life had assumed a new purpose, and this qualitative change was especially evident in his dedicated work with delinquent boys. Richard became skilled in his communications and rapport with these less advantaged boys, and he assumed some responsibilities for their educational and social well-being.

In sum, clinical sessions focused primarily on helping Richard to find meaning and direction in his day-to-day behavior. Probe questions about his background and current interests were clinical guides for clarifying his most deep-seated values and options for dealing directly with his problem of personal and social dissatisfactions.

STRATEGIES FOR CLINICAL INTERVENTIONS

Clinicians' careful consideration of clients' social class concerns in the course of their efforts to understand clients' behavior increases and enriches possibilities for successful interventions. Social class affiliations need to be thought of as determining wide ranges of behavior, which include lifestyle patterns and lifetime achievements. Although reality is ultimately incomprehensibly complex, social class allegiances can be used to explain many critical subtle and not-so-subtle differences in individual or social attitudes and actions (Smith, 1987). Therefore, considerations of social class influences are essential to a full understanding of clients' life histories, present realities, and goals.

For clinicians to accomplish this kind of assessment, the theoretical frame of reference for clinical interventions should include social class characteristics, religious affiliations, family dynamics, and gender behavior patterns (Glassner & Freedman, 1979). Only in this way can sufficient attention be given to the strength of influences of social contexts on clients' behavior. This comprehensive frame of reference extends the more microscopic perspectives conventionally used in many clinicians' analyses of interpersonal interaction.

Social class affiliations also provide clinicians with meaningful and reliable indicators of the extent to which clients conform to others' expectations. Human capacities and tendencies to conform, rather than to deviate or differentiate from others, provide significant data for assessments of problematic tendencies in dependencies, relationships, and behavior. This approach to understanding critical issues allows clinicians to build more reliable and more useful life histories than narrower perspectives permit. These data also include pertinent observations and evaluations of broad patterns of behavior throughout the courses of individual lives.

Clinicians are able to understand the complexities of social system determinants of individual social behavior, and to build effective clinical strategies based on these facts, only when they give serious consideration to such significant topics as identities, religions, families, gender, and social classes. These key phenomena and their conceptualizations represent powerful socializing influences and strong emotional dependencies in the lives of both clients and clinicians. Moreover, unless all these factors are considered in collections of life history data and formulations of directions for future action, clinical interventions will not be as effective as they could be. Broad social vantage points increase the accuracy of assessments about the most viable range of possibilities for clients' improved functioning and other life changes (Clark, 1990).

For clinicians to honor their professional responsibilities to be change agents, they must include evaluations of the social sources and social consequences of their intervention strategies. Clients increase their options and opportunities for change by seeing their personal lives in social class contexts and related public arenas, and heightening clients' awareness of the positive and negative consequences of their social class loyalties is an important stage in the slow construction of viable behavioral outcomes through clinical interventions.

10 Clinical Tasks

1. Ask clients to define their statuses in the context of their memberships in varied social classes.
2. Discuss clients' interests in lifestyles and social mobility.
3. Outline some of the advantages of living without being preoccupied with social class concerns.
4. Link social class issues to historical and evolutionary perspectives.
5. Mutually describe connections between social classes and religions.
6. Discuss clients' experiences of social classes and religions.
7. Ask clients about their personal and social goals in relation to social classes and religions.

8. Suggest ways in which clients can empower themselves through choosing particular religious or secular values to transcend their social classes.
9. Select specific values—for example, education—and show how focusing on these values can change clients' world views within religion and in society.
10. Contrast life satisfaction with accomplishing more materialistic goals related to status achievement.

Chapter 8

Culture and Religion

Religions make up a vital part of culture, and in fact are frequently referred to as the core of culture (Hechter et al., 1993). To the extent that culture is defined as the repository of societies' values, norms, and standards, religions play a primary role in culture. Religions house many of society's most sacred, and even secular, values and beliefs.

Society is possible only when there is sufficient consensus about the most crucial survival values of a given population, although the key values in different cultures exhibit varied constellations of meanings and emphases. The range of possibilities shows that cultures may be focused on traditions, on modernity, on constructive values, on destructive values, on individuals, or on collectivities. Furthermore, the nature of a society depends to a large extent on the characteristics of its dominant culture.

Both religious and cultural values give raisons d'être and substance to identities, including identities defined by race and ethnicity (Wilson, 1986). However, choices of values are not unlimited, and options have different social consequences as well as different social origins (Berger & Luckmann, 1967). Honoring the values of mainstream culture and society bestows an established status, whereas choosing peripheral, marginal values results in a less secure status (Gerth & Mills, 1953).

In many societies, traditional values derive from and are supported by established religions at the cores of these societies. For example, much of British society and of the British Empire was built on Anglican religious beliefs. In the cultures of modern industrialized societies, where secular values have become more central than traditional values, identities may be founded on either religious or cultural values. Individuals who are relatively autonomous are more able to break away from some of the restrictions of traditional values, with the result that they become respected more in their own right; that is, their diversity and differences from others are valued.

CULTURE AND SOCIETY

Cultures include mores, knowledge, beliefs, and standards, as well as norms and values. Thus cultures are essentially consensuses of social values and norms, which expedite societies' accommodations to evolutionary changes. However, the cultures of complex industrialized societies comprise many overlapping subcultures, and so they are heterogeneous rather than homogeneous, even though religions still maintain some unifying functions, for example for the purpose of defining national identity in the United States (Kosmin & Lachman, 1993).

Similarly, although most countries' cultures are uniquely distinctive, the international community must have sufficient common denominators of shared values and interests among member cultures and member societies to have meaningful communications and survive as a whole. Because both societies and their institutions are founded on cultures, cultures are necessarily human beings' primary modes of adaptation, from both national and international points of view.

Societies that change quickly, like those in some Latin American countries, are frequently based on cultures with varied subcultures that are made up of both modern and traditional values and are derived from both contemporary religions and secular sources (Beckford & Luckmann, 1989). Historically, secular values such as education, as well as religious values such as the hard work ethic of Protestantism, have precipitated modern industrial changes. Secular values, however, are particularly significant precipitators of change in cultures in which religious values have endorsed traditions, such as obedience to authority, that necessarily retarded social change (Hess, 1991).

As sources of both constructive and destructive values, cultures define the life chances of members of society. Cultures also orient members of societies to care or not to care about individuals, groups, and communities; people may be driven either by self-interest or by concern for the common good. Thus, not only do cultures provide means of adaptation, but they also are ways in which to define reality and the world. World views are vital starting points for assessing the survival and fulfillment of both individuals and societies, and identities derive from and define many of these world views.

TRADITION AND RELIGION

The essence of religion is essentially beliefs and practices, and when these are ritualized through time, they develop their own observable cultures and traditions. For example, where a given society depends on religions as sources of values, as in the Middle East, religious cultures and traditions are reflected in central societal traditions.

Tradition is an established way of sustaining social institutions. For example, religious family cultures frequently predispose their members to make commitments to specific religious communities (Johnson, 1973). Traditions also encourage characteristic habitual patterns of behavior that either promote or prevent change. These repetitions frequently become ritualistic and consequently have conservative effects on society (Luckmann, 1967). On the other hand, creative and innovative patterns of behavior precipitate change rather than merely maintain the status quo (Martin, 1990).

Religious traditions, or traditions sanctioned by religions, are usually able to exert strong influences or moral controls over both individuals and groups through respect for elders or established social conventions. Believed-in sacred powers of religion may sacralize behavior; that is, religions continue to influence apparently secular activities, such as teaching biological theories of evolution and generating related proscriptive and prescriptive principles. The content of current debates in the United States about evolution and Creationism illustrate some of the paradoxes of merging religious and secular values. Furthermore, although long-accepted civil or secular traditions, like voting, may be upheld relatively easily and effectively throughout society, issues like abortion are more intensely value-laden and in several respects depend on religious definitions of life and death for their assessment and practice.

Dangers inherent in this intimate association between significant traditions and religions include generating closed thinking, as well as creating inhibitions and restrictions in individual and group actions. However, because human behavior is by no means totally determined by these influences, actions can be changed. Value choices, which have empirical dimensions, must be carefully considered, as well as beliefs in absolute undemonstrable truths, which all too often encourage dogmatism, uncritical thinking, prejudice, discrimination, and bigotry (Wilson, 1986).

SECULARISM AND RELIGION

As societies modernize, they frequently become more secular rather than more religious (Wuthnow, 1992). To a certain extent, secularism and religion are mutually exclusive, in that if a culture is secular it cannot be religious at the same time. Middle Eastern theocracies are built on this premise. However, as societies become more industrialized, they also tend to become more pluralistic, so that secularism and religion become variously juxtaposed as compartmentalized aspects of culture and society (Yinger, 1957). Sometimes it is the tensions between secularization and religion that affect the future course of significant policy actions, such as welfare legislation (Stark & Bainbridge, 1985).

Evolutionists have speculated for more than a century that in time religion will disappear, and that all societies will gradually secularize (Durkheim, 1915). However, modern historical research has not been able to substantiate this hypothesis, and there continues to be much evidence that religion is alive and well in contemporary industrialized societies, especially in relation to American piety and religious commitment (Stark & Glock, 1968). In fact, many religions, such as Islam, have become more traditional and even more institutionalized, rather than increasingly revisionist and modern (Marty & Appleby, 1991).

Science and scientific findings are an important part of secularism in industrial societies. A more educated public has begun to demand research results to understand social conditions better, and empirical documentations of patterns of behavior at interpersonal and institutional levels of analysis are more thoroughly scrutinized and utilized than ever before. One outcome of this kind of secularization is that religious or moral questions and value issues have been demonstrated to have empirical aspects, which are more and more part of public discourse (Haught, 1984; Hess, 1991). For example, some of the side effects of malnutrition and substandard education are recognized more clearly now than in past generations. More is also known about the hazards of bringing children into the world when parents are not prepared for them emotionally or are not economically self-sufficient.

An important aspect of secularism can therefore be thought of as increased attention to the empirical dimensions of living conditions. Secular identities persist through time as well as religious identities, especially when those secular identities are associated with a valued way of doing or being (Ohnuki-Tierney, 1993). However, negative social consequences of religious beliefs may encourage members of lower classes to believe in the rewards in a heaven after death, rather than to work to achieve a more prosperous self-sufficiency in the present, even though current living conditions may be abysmal (Lenski, 1961). Empirical knowledge and some relatively newly evolved ethical standards demonstrate that all members of populations must be empowered to act in their own interests if a better world is to be established (Cornwall, 1987).

CONSTRUCTIVE VALUES AND RELIGION

Cultures necessarily consist of constructive and destructive values simultaneously, but societies frequently emphasize the importance of one kind of values or the other. Constructive values are life-enhancing, as well as conducive to increasing opportunities and resources for large numbers of people. By contrast, destructive values ultimately restrict life chances and may lead to the impairment or even destruction of many people (Hechter et al., 1993).

Constructive values usually have a direct impact on the development of human potentials. For example, God's will can be understood as being and doing the best possible, as well as making the greatest contribution to the greatest number of people. Belief in this concept can strengthen individual and collective identities as well as increase productivity. When constructive values are internalized, they become significant sources of motivation for achieving a wide variety of social improvements (Stark & Bainbridge, 1985).

Constructive values may also be related to protecting the environment, to maintaining health, and to promoting and attaining equal rights for all (Pollner, 1989). Respecting nature, rather than seeking to dominate and control environments, facilitates expressions of the greatest human potentials. For example, cherishing health and living with some degree of circumspection about daily habits and self-discipline make more prudent use of resources, and commitments to equality help to build a good society (Haney, 1989). Constructive values are therefore necessary to empower individual and social action to improve circumstances. Positive goals and ideals can be derived from religions to accomplish great things and to bring about gradual progress (Stark & Bainbridge, 1985).

DESTRUCTIVE VALUES AND RELIGION

It is easier to associate constructive than destructive values with religion, because most people have historically believed that religion is synonymous with doing good things (Beckford & Luckmann, 1989; Finke & Stark, 1992). However, in light of the many complex social changes that have resulted from industrialization and modernization, questions can be raised about the restrictive characteristics of religion, and religion can be thought of as an exploitative force that oppresses members of lower classes and the dispossessed (Hechter et al., 1993; Wuthnow, 1992).

Destructive values run counter to influences that increase opportunities and expand life chances; they distort reality and restrict activities; they inhibit the development of human potential; and they keep people in limited living conditions because they reinforce the status quo (Hunsberger, 1985). Furthermore, destructive values may be so difficult to recognize for what they are that they are frequently internalized and revered rather than avoided (Berger & Luckmann, 1967; Stark & Glock, 1968). Ultimately, destructive values are expressed in violence and warfare, which may bring about the extinction of a group or a society.

Fatalistic beliefs suggest that human beings cannot control their own destinies, and that their only choices are to accept their circumstances because they cannot be changed. For example, belief in astrology frequently reflects individual and social powerlessness, as does membership in cults. Values that uphold these kinds of beliefs inevitably limit vision and behavior, as well as keep people tied to their social statuses. Furthermore, closed belief systems may entrap whole families and communities for several generations (Barker, 1984; Bendroth, 1994).

Values that support machismo, competition, and aggression predispose individuals and groups to violent behavior. Thus societal violence can be thought of as having its roots in these specific social values; and each person has a moral responsibility to eschew the values that have destructive consequences. To the extent that religions endorse social hierarchies, religious values perpetuate inequities among members of society. However, the influences of destructive values can be minimized by not giving them attention, by refusing to internalize them as identities (Hess, 1991).

INDIVIDUAL ORIENTATION AND RELIGION

Many Western cultures, such as the United States, are individualistic in orientation and therefore correspondingly less supportive of communities and communal well-being (Herberg, 1955). In the United States, the dominant denominations of Protestantism endorse individualism through emphasizing personal contact with a deity rather than communal worship, and also through valuing individual interpretations of scriptures and religious rituals (McGuire, 1994). Mysticism, which generally has few institutional supports, is another significant influence in an individually oriented culture, as is spirituality, which largely consists of individual interpretations and expressions of communion experiences as bases for belief (Luckmann, 1967).

However, individually oriented cultures can be constructive in substance rather than destructive, and generally are more modern than traditional (Weber, 1958). Secular adaptations are characterized by wide variations in traditional religious institutions, which historically are made up of established religious beliefs, rites, and practices (Appleyard, 1993).

Religious or secular vocations—divine revelations to perform certain tasks or achieve specific goals—tend to be more commonly experienced in individually oriented cultures than in collectivity oriented societies (Weber, 1958). However, from the points of view of history and evolution, individually oriented cultures are relatively recent developments (Kaufman, 1993). There is considerable evidence to establish the fact that historically consciousness was group-oriented, with a minimal sense of individuality, and that this was a pervasively shared experience that lasted throughout the lengthy early stages of human and social development (Durkheim, 1915).

A religious concept like God's will also thrives well in individually oriented cultures (Weber, 1958). This belief suggests that personal purposes of being are dictated or revealed by a supreme deity, and that each person has a responsibility to follow this divine guidance day by day throughout life. Although God's will may be difficult to understand, and some cultural interpretations of God's will have been fatalistic (Hussain, 1984), individual initiatives for independent action may be exercised effectively through believing in God's will. Thus innovations and significant social changes are both possible and likely in individually oriented cultures (Poloma & Gallup, 1991).

COLLECTIVE ORIENTATION AND RELIGION

Societies oriented toward group concerns and community well-being do not value individual participation or contributions as much as maintaining consensus and establishing broad-scale social institutions (Kaufman, 1993). A collectivity-oriented culture is therefore qualitatively distinct from an individual-oriented culture, and frequently these become mutually exclusive through their emphases (Eisler, 1987; Hess, 1991).

To the extent that groups supersede individuals in importance in a collectivity-oriented culture, the whole becomes more than the part (Durkheim, 1915). In this way social well-being and societal functioning are frequently bought at the expense of individual well-being and functioning; wherever society counts for more than the sum of its individual members, opportunities for self-realization are necessarily severely limited (Ohnuki-Tierney, 1993).

Religions in collectivity-oriented societies frequently serve the needs of the whole of society rather than individuals, in that religion as a social institution is needed for maintaining community stability (Durkheim, 1915). Religions endorse social solidarity through their beliefs, rites, rituals, and practices, and may in fact make it very difficult for individuals to develop a strong sense of individual identity (Marty & Appleby, 1991). Thus cultures oriented to collectivities tend to produce religions that promote togetherness and traditions rather than creativity and innovation (Ellison, 1991: McGuire, 1994).

However, it is still possible for individuals to choose to strengthen their identities through internalizing religious values in collectivity-oriented cultures and societies (Mol, 1978). Although such formulations of identities may require considerable individual efforts, and an increased number of barriers may block progress to understanding and expressing identities in collectivity-oriented cultures, identity can thrive in any and all social settings (Smith, 1991). Challenges consist of moving forward for growth and empowerment in spite of innumerable social impediments (Hess, 1991).

QUESTIONS AND ANSWERS

To place the role of culture in a more objective perspective while examining the intricacies in relationships between identities and religions, two questions must be asked: "To what extent are religions the core of culture?" and "How does culture relate to identity?" Although culture includes secular norms, values, and beliefs, as well as all religions, historically moral standards have been derived primarily from religious ideals (Berger & Luckmann, 1967; Hechter et al., 1993). However, culture is the grand repository of all a society's values, and the necessary minimum degree of societal consensus is built upon culture. Therefore, within particular cultures individuals can identify with values from either sacred or secular sources, even though it is generally religious values that motivate them more strongly to accomplish what they need and want.

Because some cultures are more secular than others, an assessment must be made of the relationship between sacred and secular concerns in a particular culture by responding to the questions "What are the most important value bases of a particular culture?" and "Is a culture traditional or modern, individual-oriented or collectivity-oriented, destructive or constructive?" These considerations help to gauge the kinds of value choices individuals make and the ways in which their resulting behavior is affected by particular value choices. When options are limited, behavioral outcomes are also restricted. Nevertheless, if individuals consistently make discriminating value choices in their own interests, they are more likely to transcend the compelling pressures of conventional everyday life.

A key question that suggests the depth and dimensions of individual motivation is "In which ways do cultural world views influence behavior?" Religious values, as well as values related to secular science, are sources of how people look at themselves, others, and the universe (Haught, 1984). In most situations they see what they believe and expect what they think is possible (Berger & Luckmann, 1967; Luckmann, 1967). It is not that people are aware of what determines how they define reality, but rather that the assumptions they make about themselves and their everyday lives take charge of what they think and do in spite of themselves (Smith, 1987).

GENERALIZATIONS

A reliable starting point in assessing the influences of culture on behavior is to consider religions as the original culture of preliterate societies, and as the core of modern industrial cultures. Culture is also the primary source of values individuals choose in constructing their identities.

Cultures become increasingly complex as societies are industrialized and modernized. Some values maintain a central role in particular cultures, whereas other values become relatively marginal to mainstream concerns (Ryan, 1992). Individual value choices can ultimately move the established social locations of values, so that substantial change is accomplished rather than mere maintenance of the status quo. The most change is accomplished when peripheral values become more central—as in feminism in Western cultures—and when central values become more peripheral—as in White European cultures in the United States.

Optimally, cultural values promote open thinking and open structures to enable constructive changes to occur. Furthermore, the most viable societal adaptations are made when cultural ideals and their systems maintain some degree of flexibility. Rigid traditionalism promotes destructive values in the long run, where neither individuals nor groups can thrive. This ossification of culture eventually culminates in closure of options, reductions in possibilities for creating strong identities, and social extinction (Ashbrook, 1993).

PROPOSITIONS

Because religions form the core of cultures, religions and cultures are synonymous in several respects. The more fully the values, norms, and ideals of religions are understood, the more fully the values, norms, and ideals of culture are understood. Also, to characterize the substance of different cultures, the essence of religions must be examined.

Populations must conform to cultural values to some extent to survive. The belief systems that operate in religions make agreement and conformity more possible, and thereby assist in cultural adaptations of societies. Similarly, social institutions depend on cultural bases that include religions' standards of right and wrong, and good and evil.

Cultures are simultaneously both religious and secular, and frequently cultures polarize around extreme types; that is, behavior tends to be traditional or modern, individual-oriented or collectivity-oriented, and constructive or destructive. Furthermore, social change is related to these extremes; adaptations generally include pendulum shifts from one kind of culture to another, even though mixtures of these patterns of values exist at all times.

Science is a dominant force in the relatively recent industrialization and modernization of cultures (Haught, 1984). Technology, an outgrowth of science, speeds modernization and industrialization, and decreases the power of many social institutions and social traditions (Stark & Bainbridge, 1985). Both science and technology generate clusters of secular values that frequently motivate business successes, materialism, and the construction of other ideologies or qualities that are integral parts of contemporary cultures.

CHOICES

Culture provides a context for value choices, as well as the necessary basis for societal consensus. Culture is a meaningful context for examining identity and religion, and sets a tone for most everyday decisions. Culture strongly affects all members of society, even though they may not know it, and culture holds all the roots of individual and social agreements and disagreements.

Spiritual and religious values are generally more broad and more compelling as sources of purpose and direction than secular values. It is for this reason that spiritual and religious values can be used as guides for establishing priorities for choices of other kinds of values. People's most basic choices lie in which spiritual or religious values to select to assist them in making further cultural choices. This thinking is explored in the case of Robert, later in this chapter.

Specific social trends follow in the wake of individual and collective value choices. Individual choices of modern values gradually move society toward being secular and industrialized (Kosmin & Lachman, 1993). Choices of collectivity-oriented values encourage the formation of communities in society and other meaningful groups. Choices of constructive values decrease destruction in society and may eventually bring about positive qualitative changes. Thus, each sort of choice has a marked impact on society. Choices necessarily either support the status quo or create new kinds of consensus and innovative social forms, and in the long run cultural evolution moves societies either toward viable adaptations or extinction (Teilhard de Chardin, 1965).

CASE STUDY

Robert Smith was a 35-year-old African American unable to complete a college degree or find a satisfactory job. He had been raised by his mother, a single parent, and he was Roman Catholic in religion and education. Robert sought therapy to help him to achieve more education before he became too old to change.

Several members of Robert's family were Protestant, including an emotionally significant great aunt who had cared for him for much of his childhood. He gravitated toward her at this time of crisis, because he suspected that he might gain more from following her religion than by dutifully trying to duplicate his mother's. Robert also suspected that he might have more interest in education if his religious beliefs could be sharper and more meaningful.

Much to his mother's surprise and dismay, Robert decided to convert to Protestantism. He also enrolled in a local community college and put himself on a track that would lead to a degree in finance. He wanted to have a career in accounting, and he thought this kind of education would serve him well in preparing for this field.

Robert's mother continued to be distressed at these changes in Robert. However, Robert was able to sustain a fairly close relationship with her in spite of her upset. He also spent more time than usual with different members of her family, and they also became sources of guidance for him in making these major decisions about the future.

Robert was able to reverse some of his earlier devaluing of education. Protestantism heightened his sense of individuality, and he no longer felt guilty about not following the rules of the Roman Catholic religion. He did not like to displease his mother by not being faithful to the tenets of Roman Catholicism, but in fact, after several months, when Robert's mother saw how much his changes had improved his life, she started to question some aspects of her own Roman Catholic faith.

Analysis

Robert was able to make these rather dramatic changes in his life because he realized that to raise his status in society he would have at least to complete a college education. Although initially he had difficulty resolving his dependency issues with his mother—she was very close to him emotionally because she was his only parent—his contacts with his great aunt helped him to break out of his mother's direct influence.

Robert's decision to convert to Protestantism was evidence that he was beginning to think for himself and to see connections between his religious beliefs, religious practices, functioning, and productivity. He believed that he could achieve more if he took charge of these important parts of his life in his own way.

Robert increased his autonomy by following his own values of education and professional accomplishment. Long-standing spiritual interests also led him to change his religious affiliation. Although his conversion was not very formal, this shift in orientation seemed to increase meaning in his life, and he was better able to concentrate on planning a satisfactory career.

Robert's great aunt was a great support in his decision making. She also provided a buffer between him and his mother. By getting back in touch with other family members, Robert strengthened his functioning position. Furthermore, his broader view of society meant that he could deal with authority figures and hierarchies in the education system more effectively than he had been able to at a younger age.

Thus Robert kept his individuality intact, in spite of many family members' encroachments on his privacy. He maintained his spiritual beliefs in his new religious home of Protestantism, and he benefitted from the support of these additional community contacts. Although he made much clinical progress in a 6-month period, he decided to continue consultations to gain further guidance for pursuing his career.

STRATEGIES FOR CLINICAL INTERVENTIONS

The most successful clinical interventions must include serious considerations of the effects and continuities of cultural influences as well as small-scale dynamics. Because the concept of culture is fairly global and versatile, it can be applied to subgroups in society as well as to society at large. For clinical purposes, culture provides a full context for understanding clients' dilemmas and behaviors. For example, specific kinds of subcultures locate individuals in the context of values and help to define the ways in which they make their value choices and express their priorities (Cornwall, 1987).

Cultures assist in establishing the equilibrium necessary for societal survival and viability by holding the polarities of value differences in creative tension with each other. Cultures have their own sense of wholeness, which facilitates coherence and meaning as well as shared values, and they are more advantageous as open systems than as closed. Clinicians and clients can benefit from understanding these varied qualities of cultures, because cultures frame the choices and options clients have in reestablishing their identities and participating in complex social changes. Clinicians must also know how to encourage clients to participate in constructive rather than destructive individual and cultural changes, whatever the qualities of their own particular culture or subculture (Berger & Luckmann, 1967).

Religion and spirituality are prisms through which clinicians can see clients' cultures and value choices more clearly. For example, clinicians can understand the options available to their clients more easily if they assess the cultural contexts of their clients in relation to concepts such as doing God's will in both religious and secular settings (Ellison, 1991). Understanding the cultural contexts of clients' value choices also increases clinicians' abilities to trace the consequences of particular selections in relation to social traditions and innovations. Any kind of spiritual or religious motivation has both individual and social secular consequences as well as qualitative spiritual and religious effects, depending on the kinds of values clients internalize. Thus, because there are secular underpinnings to every religious belief and practice, clinicians also need to be able to assess the impact of these influences on clients' clinical progress and their everyday behavior (Luckmann, 1967). If clinicians ignore the strength of the effects of culture, spirituality, and religion on clients' behavior, their interventions will be less consequential in their clients' lives, and less effective in promoting constructive changes in the long run (Hall, 1986a, 1986b, 1991; Hunsberger, 1985; Pollner, 1989; Randour, 1993).

10 Clinical Tasks

1. Direct clinical discussions to the topic of religions and values in the context of culture.
2. Help clients assess the cultural significance of value choices in their everyday lives.
3. Describe cultural influences in religious practices and social roles.
4. Analyze the importance of traditions in cultures and society, as well as in clients' lives.
5. Discuss the significance of modern values for clients' religious and secular beliefs and practices.
6. Contrast individual-oriented and collectivity-oriented cultures in clients' lives.
7. Contrast constructive and destructive values in clients' religious and cultural experiences.
8. Show clients how cultural influences can be neutralized or minimized through autonomous value choices.
9. Assess the impact of secularism in clients' lives.
10. Support clients' definitions and actions toward goals that transcend cultural imperatives.

Chapter 9

Responsibility and Religion

Most religions and themes of spirituality raise issues about whether human beings are responsible moral agents in their own right, or whether their behavior is more or less determined by animal instincts, divine will, or fate (Gerth & Mills, 1953). Assessments about the extent to which people choose their destinies and control their life situations or life chances grow out of assumptions about whether supernatural powers are responsible for human behavior, or whether people are fully responsible for what they do (Berger & Luckmann, 1967).

Deliberations on these themes are useful for deepening understanding about identities and ways in which identities influence behavior. The concept of identity relates directly to the principle of responsibility, in that clinical data show how strengthened identity increases awareness of responsibilities (Bowen, 1978). However, sometimes strengthening one's identity may make it more difficult to be fully responsible because one's standards of behavior are elevated by this strengthening (Mol, 1978).

Understanding how ethical decisions influence behavior is another aspect of responsibility (Ashbrook, 1993; Haught, 1984). Facts also influence experiences of religion and definitions of responsibility, with the result that facts and moral or ethical issues are inextricably related (Glassner & Freedman, 1979). Therefore, people need to be concerned about the many individual and social consequences of their actions, rather than have blind faith in supernatural powers or godheads without paying attention to results (Ellison, 1991).

More issues emerge when the interactions between religion and responsibility are examined. Although it is fairly easy to acknowledge that beliefs guide and influence actions, it is difficult to discern which beliefs are most pertinent to individual and social interests, and why responsibilities should be taken seriously, especially because it frequently appears to be possible—and even beneficial—to live unreflectively and at the same time achieve life satisfaction or contribute to the common good.

RESPONSIBILITY

Responsibility includes strengthening human abilities to respond compassionately and constructively in any situation, rather than negatively and thoughtlessly. Thoughtful behavior is generally more responsible than automatic reactivity. Moral definitions of responsibility include dealing intelligently and ethically with particular circumstances, as well as with consequences that flow from decisions made and behavior undertaken. Responsibility also relates to capacities to define goals and objectives that are congruent with both individual integrity and the social good.

Responsibility is an aspect of every moment of every waking hour, because all thoughts and actions have consequences of some kind. Responsibilities cannot be escaped, and most given living situations need to be improved. A person who strengthens identity also increases his or her responsibility. By clarifying goals and ideals, such a person engages in more enlightened action, which benefits both self and others. Thus, achieving personal autonomy requires defining responsibility in relation to religious and secular beliefs, past and present (Hammond, 1992).

Responsibilities are inspired and developed by families, religions, social classes, education, politics, and other social agencies (Pollner, 1989). The substance of myriad responsible or irresponsible individual contributions necessarily feeds into the core of society, culture, and social institutions, because meeting social needs is necessary for the survival of all societies and the world system. Although people frequently associate heroic acts with being responsible, generally speaking responsibility refers just as much—if not more—to series of mundane daily tasks rather than to spectacular feats. Deciding to send a child to college, for example, and tackling all the work it entails, may be more responsible than dealing with a particular social problem like homelessness.

Responsible behavior is connected to and flows from individuals' deepest, most cherished values. People become higher selves, or stronger selves, when they are responsible in their decisions and actions. Merely reacting to others—that is, being governed by primarily by feelings rather than by knowledge of what is optimal—leads to less productive behavior and fewer constructive contributions to others; emotional reactivity frequently precludes or restricts the ability to see possibilities.

RELIGIOUS RESPONSIBILITY

Religious responsibility can be thought of as obligations or duties that respond to supernatural powers. That is, being religiously responsible requires meeting expectations that are defined by understanding supernatural powers and how people are intended to live in accordance with these powers. Thus religious responsibility implies a particular relationship with supernatural powers, as well as specific qualities in relationships with others. However, some religious obligations, such as the ideal of spending much time studying the Torah in Orthodox Judaism, may seem far removed from everyday realities.

Religious responsibility differs from secular responsibility in that religious responsibility is upheld by sacred rather than secular sanctions. Furthermore, whether or not people decide to follow what they understand to be their religious responsibilities, they gain more meaning and satisfaction by following what they believe are spiritual dictates than by merely conforming to secular roles. Thus, both spirituality and religions are valuable resources for problem solving and coping (Pargament et al., 1988).

Religious responsibility transports people beyond their immediate empirical concerns. When they identify themselves as religious or spiritual beings, they simultaneously transcend their immediate surroundings and become more able to use both their human and spiritual capacities. For example, thinking of themselves as children of God releases people's human, if not divine, potentials. Furthermore, aligning themselves or their identities with divine sources enables people to meet their religious and secular responsibilities without arduous efforts or regrets, even though sometimes the moral essences of identities may precipitate behavior that seems dramatically out of character (Malony & Southard, 1992).

Religious responsibility can be thought of in relation to a specific religion—which may be either a denomination or a sect—or it can be considered as a spiritual mandate that transcends all religions as well as all secular conditions (Poloma & Gallup, 1991). When people follow what they believe to be divine inspiration, their identities, visions, decisions, and actions are strongly influenced by their understanding of that source, and by their particular religious or spiritual beliefs (Van Zandt, 1991).

MORAL CONCERNS

Moral concerns, such as eradicating injustices, put humans in touch with their basic collective needs and with institutional means of survival. The mores of a group or society are established patterns of behavior that lead toward that group's or society's adaptation and continuity, rather than to extinction.

As people mature, they grow increasingly aware that their existence depends in part on support from the society and groups to which they belong, rather than solely on their individual efforts. Optimally, they recognize their interdependence in personal, professional, and political milieus, as well as their intrinsic human and spiritual characteristics. Individuals can only survive and live fully when they make deliberate efforts to meet some of the basic needs and moral concerns of the groups and societies to which they belong.

Moral concerns add a vital dimension to mundane daily concerns. Thriving satisfactorily is not achieved by thinking and acting primarily in relation to individual goals. All human beings must find ways to incorporate their individually oriented activities with behavior that meets others' needs and extends social mores toward societal survival and adaptation. For example, unless violence against all women is halted, individual women are not free. Only in these ways can personal satisfaction and fulfillment be gained, and human potential developed, because personal integrity is inextricably tied to sustaining significant social values (Tillich, 1952).

Moral concerns are differentially related to families, religions, social classes, cultures, education, and political systems, as well as to societies. However, these different social contexts serve similar functions of linking individual identities to broad patterns of behavior. For example, individuals become responsible community members or responsible members of society, rather than merely responsible family members. Because identities have broad social sources or bases, people are unable to live meaningfully in isolation. They are necessarily moral agents in all aspects of their lives, and not merely human animals.

ETHICAL ISSUES

Ethical issues focus thinking, decision making, and behavior more clearly on social beliefs about what is right and wrong than on survival concerns. Thus ethical issues are components of the broader moral concerns of society, and they become moral concerns through their many diverse social consequences. For example, in professional decisions about medical ethics, individual well-being is bound to others' well-being through shared values and needs. Furthermore, because individual survival is ultimately inextricably related to the survival of society, ideally each person must deal with both broad moral concerns and more specific ethical issues.

Standards of right and wrong lie at the heart of ethical issues, and historically these cultural priorities have derived from religious rather than secular values (Hechter et al., 1993). However, because of rapid industrialization, secular values have sometimes diminished the salience and centrality of religious values in societies' cultures and individuals' identities. In many situations of rapid social change, traditions appear to be largely dissolved by newly emerging modern ways of doing things (Smith, 1991). Consequently, ethical issues are frequently defined as relative and situational, such as in legal concerns, rather than as being based on absolutes derived from past traditions (McNamara, 1992; Wuthnow, 1992).

Ethical issues can be discerned in any given set of circumstances. As moral agents, human beings must continuously predict and assess the best, most appropriate things to do. Although people may or may not be aware of all the ethical dilemmas and choices that are integral parts of their daily lives, ethical issues are nevertheless constantly present and inescapable.

Strengthening individual identities increases familiarity with the ubiquitousness of ethical issues (Hall, 1986b; Mol, 1987). Also, when identities are strong, actions based on integrity are more predictable and more consistent than when there is no clear sense of identity (Hall, 1990a). Thus, religions and religious values can guide ethical choices to increase the moral well-being of both societies and individuals (Cornwall, 1987; Kaufman, 1993; Pollner, 1989).

EMPIRICAL DATA AND RELIGION

Historically, empirical data have been thought of as contradicting or opposing religions, in that data necessarily refer to material realities and concerns, rather than to spirit or to beliefs in supernatural forces. For example, the development of science challenged many religious beliefs, particularly religious explanations of the creation of the universe. However, distinctions between specific religious belief systems can be documented by defining and recording the empirical associations and consequences of varied sets of beliefs (Poloma & Gallup, 1991). A particular religion, such as Roman Catholicism, or a particular belief system, such as atheism, can be documented as having constructive or destructive individual and social consequences by examining related empirical data (Hunsberger, 1985; Lenski, 1961; Yinger, 1957). Clinical data can also be used to make this kind of evaluation of the influence of religions, belief systems, and spirituality on everyday decision making and interaction (Randour, 1993).

To the extent that religions are made up of relatively closed belief systems about truths that are considered to be absolute, facts may serve to open up those beliefs by proving or disproving the truths (Roof, 1992). Being willing to disprove religious truths opens thought systems rather than perpetuates dogmas and closed doctrines (Hammond, 1992; Kaufman, 1993). Furthermore, it is individual conscience rather than dogma or doctrine that directs or motivates responsible action (McNamara, 1992). In a similar vein, science breaks through traditions and religions, in that scientific hypotheses are proved or disproved through facts rather than supported by beliefs alone (Haught, 1984).

Being honest about facts facilitates the discovery of important differences between those religious truths that work positively for people and those that limit individual and social contributions (Pargament et al., 1988; Randour, 1993). Ignoring facts closes off empirical realities, so that religions become so far removed from the everyday world that they can no longer guide behavior effectively (Barker, 1984). The usefulness of religions is related to the ways in which religions inspire people, expand consciousness, and guide behavior toward achievements for the social good rather than for individual goals (Schumaker, 1992). Empirical data help to asses differences among the many ways possible to contribute to society (Smith, 1987); without this kind of reliable check on reality, people would not be able to express themselves as authentically (Glassner & Freedman, 1979).

EMPIRICAL DATA AND RESPONSIBILITY

To be fully responsible, individuals must anticipate and account for the empirical consequences of their decisions and actions sufficiently and accurately. This is necessary because people cannot afford to ignore the moral impact of their actions on individuals and society (McGuire, 1994). Responsibility consists largely in making distinctions between empirical consequences that are constructive and those that are destructive.

Gathering facts about any situation increases one's objectivity about options, which itself may contrast sharply with merely doing what feels right. For example, unequal life conditions must be documented and demonstrated before one can make appropriate and effective contributions to the common good. Only by understanding differential advantages and disadvantages can one construct compassionate policies that meet real needs.

Empirical data can also be used advantageously to substantiate everyday trial and error activities. Although no one can escape experiencing both satisfactory and unsatisfactory situations, discovering which consequences result from specific decisions and actions helps to avoid unnecessary unpleasantness. Thus factual knowledge improves possibilities for making wise judgments. Facts suggest which track is right or wrong; they illuminate ways in which people habitually fool themselves; and they break through myths and other kinds of false consciousness that harbor dangerous delusions and illusions.

Although formal empirical research is not needed to assess pertinent facts about specific situations, it is only through examining facts that accurate assessments about responsibilities can be made. For example, sufficient facts must be grasped for individuals to see the big picture of personal responsibility and religious affiliation (Lenski, 1961). Thus, moral issues cannot be sufficiently understood through closed belief systems or through value systems that do not include considerations of facts and related findings. Understanding the realities of social contexts increases constructive rather than destructive attitudes and actions toward self and others (Berger & Luckmann, 1967).

IDENTITY AND RESPONSIBILITY

Having strong identities necessarily leads people to becoming more responsible moral agents. Identity and responsibility are inextricably related; strong identity increases awareness of individual potential and social concerns. Furthermore, it is only by seeing what can be done to support others, and how to contribute to their needs, that people become fully responsible (Wuthnow, 1991).

Behaving automatically, which results from having very little sense of identity, is not effective in attaining individual goals or in consolidating collective efforts to make substantial contributions to society. Thus vigilantly creating and sustaining identities is a necessary precondition for acting responsibly at all times. One advantage of religious over secular values in defining identity is that their believed-in sacredness gives them additional power and influence over behavior (Smith, 1991). Religions call forth considerations of ultimate concerns for survival and fulfillment, and it is only through these broadest contexts that the most responsible decisions about current actions can be made (Tillich, 1952).

Facts related to individual beliefs help to define people's abilities to respond meaningfully to given situations. Indeed, identities cannot be nurtured, nor responsibilities met, if sufficient attention is not given to empirical realities. Thus specific beliefs and values predictably bring with them real and significant consequences for relationships and actions, especially in relation to individual achievements. Knowing facts about particular situations deepens understanding about related moral concerns and ethical issues, and leads to fuller expressions of integrity (Gerth & Mills, 1953).

QUESTIONS AND ANSWERS

A basic question already raised in this discussion of religion and responsibility is "Are people responsible moral agents in their own right?" To answer this query entails examining issues such as "To what extent is behavior determined by animal instincts, divine will, or fate?" and "Do people choose their own destinies?" and "Are people fully in control of their own lives?" Although these questions may be largely unanswerable, contemplating them deepens understanding of what it means to be responsible moral agents. They help people clarify where responsibilities begin and end, as well as ascertain how both under- and overresponsibility easily become irresponsibility.

In assessing the whole picture of responsibility and religion, another question that arises is "What is the range of religious and secular responsibilities that must be considered?" People benefit from recognizing that their families, religions, social classes, education, and political systems make different demands on their time and energy, and that appropriate definitions of responsibilities and enlightened action are needed in all these social spheres if they are to survive, be fulfilled, and make worthwhile contributions to society. Moral integrity consists largely in balancing these kinds of varied demands and responsibilities; individuals cannot choose to be responsible merely in single areas of their lives if they are to live up to their potentials as moral beings.

A question that further clarifies the relationship between identity and responsibility is "To what extent do empirical data define responsibilities?" To be fully responsible, individuals must monitor the consequences of their actions. This process allows them to ascertain whether specific contributions are in fact supportive and constructive, or destructive. When their identities are strengthened, individuals' responsible behavior in both personal and public life is increased, and empirical data can assist them in renewing or changing commitments so as to meet responsibilities more effectively (Wuthnow, 1991).

GENERALIZATIONS

Being a moral agent is the essence of being human in the fullest sense. To be an effective moral agent, one must be consistently responsible for one's actions. Thus, being a true moral agent requires making integrity the highest priority at all times. Furthermore, because human beings are spiritual as well as physical, emotional, and mental, moral agency is the most vital characteristic of identities.

Historically, religions have been the primary sources for models of moral agency as well as for moral values. Codes of moral conduct and religious virtues, as well as spiritual leadership and prophecy, provide guides for what it means to be a moral agent. Value choices must be made in each situation that arises; these choices must be made to emulate or deny the moral power of these examples.

Making deliberate value choices heightens people's awareness of moral imperatives, and people with strong identities are stronger moral agents than people with weak identities. Society benefits from individuals' moral growth as well as the individuals themselves, because when people become more active moral agents, they do their best to meet collective needs rather than individualistic agendas.

Thus the sources and bases of both identity and responsibility are at the same time religious and moral (Hammond, 1992). These sources are also essentially social rather than individual in character; human beings have moral as well as dependency ties to the whole of society. People cannot be fulfilled merely as individuals, unless they honor others' concerns as well as their own.

PROPOSITIONS

The more identities are strengthened through value choices, the more individual and social responsibilities are increased (Mol, 1978). Being responsible increases one's effectiveness as a moral agent, and being a full human being is inextricably related to being an effective moral agent. As they have historically, religions continue to serve as the most significant and powerful source of values and meanings for this important empowerment as human and moral agencies.

Being responsible includes being open-minded and flexible in interpersonal and social relationships. To stay aware of sacred presence and guidance, or to be truly enlightened by secular sources, individuals must expunge formulas and dogmas; responsibility means that self must be sufficiently developed so as to refrain from being dogmatic and authoritarian in relationships and patterns of interaction. The more open and flexible social negotiations are, the more responsible acts will be in the long run.

As well as being reliable guides in everyday decision making, empirical data suggest a variety of ways to be responsible. Religious and spiritual values alone are insufficient sources of inspiration and motivation for action; actual behavioral consequences must continuously be assessed. Furthermore, because empirical realities can be ignored or denied only at peril, responsible individuals pay attention to the empirical dimensions and consequences of their actions.

Living reflectively and behaving responsibly rather than irresponsibly enhances life satisfaction. People benefit directly to the extent that they take their responsibilities seriously, and others also predictably benefit indirectly or directly if their actions are truly responsible (Haney, 1989).

CHOICES

People are responsible, or become responsible, because they exercise free will in their religious and secular choices. Religions frequently prescribe moral obligations to follow sacred dictates, to live in divine presence, or to develop particular talents and skills as divine beings. The impact of these kinds of precepts and moral dictates hinges on human beings' willingness and ability to incorporate particular values in their behavior. Free will, whether or not it is divinely ordained, ultimately necessitates that people make many difficult value and moral choices in the course of their daily lives.

Being responsible necessarily includes recognizing the ethical dimensions of all situations. Responsible decision making is therefore by no means confined to major turning points or important events, but rather is called forth in dealing with any individual circumstances or social conditions. People exist because they are able to make choices, and they are who they are because of their choices. Otherwise stated, people act according to the moral essences they select as their identities. Optimally, their choices are based on empirical realities as well as on specific values. People need to analyze the implications of their overlapping responsibilities, and ideally their future choices will be made in light of the empirical consequences of their most cherished values.

Because the empirical underpinnings of moral principles and ethical dictates cannot be dismissed or denied without penalty, individuals must find ways to express deep-seated beliefs responsibly. It is because of these correlations that exercising responsibility pays rich dividends of personal and social fulfillment, and enhances individual contributions to others. This is true in the case that follows, in which a young woman struggled with her definition of responsibility and religion.

CASE STUDY

Sonia Lee was a 26-year-old Chinese woman having difficulty building personal relationships and adjusting to her cultural heritage. Born in China, Sonia had come to live in the United States when she was 6 years old. Although she had many family members in China, she had not returned there, and she still lived with her parents and sister in a suburb of Washington, DC.

Sonia's family tried to practice the Taoist religion, but this was a difficult enterprise within the culture of the United States. The Lees had Chinese friends who shared their beliefs, but they did not have the equivalent of a Taoist community. Sonia's education demanded much adaptation to American culture, and she felt alienated from her family and the Chinese and Taoist cultures.

Sonia sought clinical intervention to help her to resolve some of her uncomfortable and distressing dating issues. Also, she was unsure of where her responsibility lay with regard to her current family relationships. She suffered from depression and confusion, as well as a lack of confidence in building friendships, especially with men. Although she had fairly strong intellectual interests in Chinese culture and Taoism, it was hard for her to feel rooted in these traditions.

Sonia was able to follow a course of therapy that reconnected her to her ethnic heritage. She met more people of her own age group by attending cultural functions associated with her Chinese and Taoist interests, and she gained self-confidence by concentrating efforts on constructing a more authentic identity for herself. She spent more time with her parents, sister, and some other family members, and began to investigate ways in which she could return to China for a visit.

Analysis

Sonia's personal and relationship symptoms resulted largely from losing touch with her extended family connections and deep cultural roots. Much of Sonia's discomfort was also related to feelings of overresponsibility for the well-being of her parents and sister. Her incapacity to build friendships resulted from her lack of self-confidence, which derived from her confused sense of identity.

Sonia started to make progress in her social life when she became sufficiently curious about her ethnic origins that studying Chinese cultural history and gathering information about her Chinese extended family became compelling projects. Furthermore, Sonia decided to get the information she needed for her own education in these areas by experimenting with social experiences, rather than merely pursuing this quest in intellectual ways. That is, she went to cultural events to build a network of Chinese acquaintances and friends for herself, rather than to the library to get documented source materials.

Sonia's initiative in this quest changed her functioning position in her immediate nuclear family. She became more autonomous and less reactive to her parents and sister, and at the same time she stopped trying so hard to assimilate into American groups. Although she continued to pursue many of her American interests, she made sure that she did not raise her expectations unrealistically high about being accepted fully by these groups.

In the course of therapy Sonia made plans to further reconnect herself with her Chinese heritage. Studies of Taoism inspired her to create a big picture of her life, as well as a philosophy, and she was able to withstand some of the pernicious influences of American culture through undertaking this venture. Although Sonia did not find a man she wanted to marry during the period of her clinical work, she became much more active socially than she had been before, and her depressions disappeared. Her confusion was also dispelled, and she began to move forward into her future with heightened senses of clarity and identity.

STRATEGIES FOR CLINICAL INTERVENTIONS

Some of the most effective clinical work includes strategies for clients to construct moral philosophies (Pargament et al., 1988). When critical individual or social problems uproot the foundations of clients' beliefs, and their habitual styles of problem solving are no longer viable, clients must find or forge new ways to understand realities. One technique is for clinicians to focus their questioning and discussions on clients' value choices, and on the empirical consequences of the particular value choices their clients have made.

Helping clients to define their senses of responsibility is another worthwhile goal for clinical interventions. Although this aim may not necessarily be articulated as a priority by clients themselves, or by clinicians during preliminary clinical exchanges—which are necessarily taken up with stress reduction concerns—for purposes of long-term changes, issues of responsibility must eventually be addressed (Bowen, 1978).

Discussing spirituality, religions, or religious values is frequently an effective way to initiate clinical dialogue on the value-laden topic of responsibility. It is imperative that clinicians discover how clients define responsibility in their own lives, rather than influence clients to accept clinicians' definitions. In fact, a crucial clinical goal is for clinicians assiduously to avoid imposing their standards of responsibility and related beliefs on clients.

Dialogue about values may be usefully focused on secular matters such as family responsibilities, gender expectations, social class lifestyles, education, and politics. These exchanges need to be profoundly analytical rather than superficial, and optimally clinicians should use these kinds of discussions as opportunities to tap into clients' most significant priorities, interests, and concerns. Furthermore, a certain amount of this kind of self-knowledge is a necessary starting point for future responsible decision making and meaningful action (McNamara, 1992).

10 Clinical Tasks

1. Invite clients to define and understand alternative definitions of responsibility.
2. Relate clients' views of responsibility to their religious contexts.
3. Discuss ways in which religions have influenced clients' definitions of responsibilities.

4. Outline how clients can become more aware of the moral dilemmas that exist in their everyday lives.
5. Discuss the importance of empirical consequences in assessing individual and social responsibilities.
6. Examine some of the specific empirical consequences of clients' actions in their regular reports of behavior at clinical sessions.
7. Link experiential data to clients' beliefs and value choices.
8. Assist clients in planning strategies to increase the responsibility they assume for their actions.
9. Define moral and ethical issues in the choices clients make.
10. Support clients in projects and plans to increase responsibility for their value choices and behavior.

Chapter 10

Social Change and Religion

Historically, religions have served as both conservative forces and catalysts for change. In their capacities as repositories of meanings, religions can motivate large numbers of individuals—even whole populations—either to sustain traditions or to reformulate goals and ideals and do things differently (Lenski, 1951). Moreover, it is only through using a broad historical perspective that people can sufficiently understand the depth and scope of religious influences, and the strength of their impact on the quantity and quality of social life and social change (Ashbrook, 1993).

Religious differences have caused violently destructive battles in many times and places (Eisler, 1987). This destruction is linked to religions because abstractions and rigidities in belief systems frequently generate dogmas that provoke disputes and conflicts (Finke & Stark, 1992). It is this kind of bigotry that accentuates religious differences so much that they become irretrievably contradictory and incompatible, with the result that national and international disagreements may escalate into overt conflict and warfare (Eisler, 1987; Lerner, 1986).

Religions can be thought of as consisting of those beliefs that are both individually and socially experienced as sacred (Wuthnow, 1992). Although it is crucial to forge identities through basing actions on uniqueness, and through expressing specific values of meaningful groups, there is also a point at which it is important deliberately to identify with the whole human race. For example, although it may be meaningful to identify with all women, it is also morally significant to conduct behavior according to membership in humankind. Although many people realize that there is no escape from the human condition, and that biology knows few cultural or status differences, these universal characteristics and realities have to be actively acknowledged for people to identify with the whole human race. Even where nation states no longer completely define citizens' everyday circumstances, as they did in the 18th century, awareness of their membership in the world community must be cultivated—an awareness that in fact is facilitated by modern scientific and technological advances (Appleyard, 1993). Group moral agencies such as religions or even political parties may be prime movers of change, but individuals and groups must recognize and accept their responsibilities for the implementation and consequences of the particular changes they initiate.

RELIGION AS A CONSERVATIVE FORCE

To the extent that religions reflect core social values, such as reverence for social status and social hierarchies, they play important roles in maintaining the status quo of any society. Religions also sanctify life passages, as well as provide ready-made but correspondingly limited identities for their worshippers, especially for women (Daly, 1968), and create senses of fulfillment and satisfaction, which may sometimes be false. For example, when positive feelings derive largely from acting in accordance with tradition, religious dictates such as conforming to community rituals may actually decrease rather than increase opportunities for change. Furthermore, the maximum scope of changes made through these kinds of conservative religious mechanisms in both modern and preliterate societies includes usually no more than individual adjustments and social adaptations (Ashbrook, 1993).

Religions may both unite nations in wartime and provide bases for interfaith or ethnic conflicts, as they have done recently in Northern Ireland and Bosnia. Religions frequently foster a high degree of unity among their adherents, as in preliterate religions and Islam, which tends to perpetuate already existing social forms and processes, rather than lead to expressions of individuality and creativity (Durkheim, 1915). Furthermore, religions have so many pervasive visible and invisible influences that their impact is difficult to define, locate, or assess (Luckmann, 1967). In fact, the worship of supernatural powers or godheads can be thought of as modes of obeisance to society at large, where sacred values epitomize the primary standards and ideals of the mainstream population (Durkheim, 1915).

Whenever religions successfully recruit members of the youngest generations of families, traditional structures and rituals tend to be perpetuated. Religious denominations such as Protestantism, Roman Catholicism, and Judaism have powerful institutionalized ways to socialize young children. Passing on established ways of doing things is achieved by performing ritualistic repetitions of religious practices, which ensure that very little change occurs within or among those traditions. However, there may be considerable variation among subcultures of the same society, such as among different racial and ethnic groups, and this diversity of practices can inspire changes other than adaptations (Wilson, 1986).

One problem related to these functions of religion as a conservative force in society is that religions may increase the possibility for ossification of rituals and institutions that support society, such as families and political systems. Wherever there is widespread rote repetition, as in ritualized class behavior in England, social stagnation rather than innovation occurs, and societies tend not to be able to prosper or transform themselves (Ebaugh, 1993). Furthermore, overly conservative social influences of religions can lead toward societal extinction in the long run, as was the case with some nineteenth-century religious sects that practiced sexual purity through celibacy rather than allowing procreation.

RELIGION AND INNOVATION

New, different, or rapidly evolving religions frequently serve as sources of ideals and values to promote change, sometimes manifesting themselves as liberation theologies, radical religions, or social movements (Smith, 1991). The beliefs of some religious sects, such as Unity Christianity, may present alternative world views, as well as distinctively different definitions of human nature. Thus traditional ideals and values may be expanded to include broadened ranges of possibilities for worship and social action. In fact, the future of religions themselves may ultimately depend on the interplay of the trends of secularization, revivalism, and cult formation (Stark & Bainbridge, 1985).

When people come to believe, with passion and faith, that certain ideals are worth pursuing, their behavior changes, and they can have more impact on social structures. This phenomenon is recorded in varied research on utopianism (Manuel & Manuel, 1979). For example, if individuals or groups believe that they are following divine dictates, or doing God's will, they enter into courses of action with increased zeal and commitment to accomplish what they consider to be God-given specific goals. Thus effective social movements are frequently fueled by religious fervor (Lorentzen, 1991).

Although some new or different religious ideals may be counterproductive, or even destructive, in their social consequences, they frequently engender suggestions or strategies for improvements of the human condition (Hess, 1991). However, the long-range betterment of the human condition requires assessing the relative impacts of science and religion, as well as understanding the human quest for purpose (Haught, 1984). When people feel that they are moral agents in their own right, they are more able to accomplish noble goals that reflect the common good than if they believe that they are pawns of a meaningless fate

(Weber, 1958). Furthermore, even secular goals then take on tones of moral purposefulness, especially when they are related to national identity and related social meanings (Ohnuki-Tierney, 1993).

Thus individuals who pray or meditate for guidance can be more heroic in their actions than if they feel that they are acting completely independently or in isolation from the needs of others (Hunsberger, 1985; Wuthnow, 1991). Through prayer and meditation they develop more of a sense of being connected with the whole of life, and with supernatural forces, than if they assume that their actions start and finish with themselves (Butterworth, 1969). This sense of connectedness is an empirical manifestation of human and evolutionary dependencies (Teilhard de Chardin, 1965), and it is this kind of conscious, socially based confidence that motivates the most consistent and effective patterns of action, which ultimately bring about innovation and amelioration on a broad scale (Blasi, 1991).

RELIGION AND HISTORY

Because religions are basic social institutions, they are essential to the functioning of society as a whole (Macionis & Benokraitis, 1995). It is because religions are necessary for social adaptations that they are ever-present influences in historical changes (Martin, 1990). Religious beliefs, rituals, and organizations cannot be subtracted from everyday social exchanges, and they remain as important determinants of history, whatever the degree of secularization of a given society (Berger & Luckmann, 1967).

Religions have played significant roles in history and social change in many varied ways (Finke & Stark, 1992). For example, the quest for religious freedom led to the founding of the United States, the Crusades kept Muslims out of Spain and enforced the spread of Christianity, and religious differences have exacerbated current warfare in Bosnia. Also, in recent years, Protestantism has been an increasingly important influence in the development of Latin America (Martin, 1990). Thus, as well as being integral parts of diverse cultural beliefs in societies, religions have served as rallying points for conflicts and sometimes wars (Yinger, 1957). Paradoxically, both the unifying and the divisive powers of religions have been evident in many different battles throughout history (Beckford & Luckmann, 1989). History emphasizes the importance of political leaders and military forces, many of whom are known to have been religiously motivated (Lerner, 1986). Religions, through both their everyday and political crisis applications, are significant parts of history and have consequences for society as a whole, as well as reflect the spiritual styles of particular cohorts, such as members of the post-World War II baby boom in the United States (Roof, 1992).

In assessing the overall impact of religious influences on population masses, one tentative but frequently drawn conclusion is that religions can promote false consciousness and therefore discourage people from acting in their own real interests (Bendroth, 1994). That is, religions are viewed as forces that keep less powerful populations and social classes in subjugated positions for long periods of time by preventing the impetus for changes based on actual conditions (Collins, 1990). Where religions are used by the powerful few to control the masses, it is the vested interests of the power wielders that are sustained, rather than the more general interests of the members of the lower social classes (Beckford & Luckmann, 1989).

RELIGION AND EVOLUTIONARY ADAPTATION

Religions are repositories of social mores as well as of spiritual values. From an evolutionary point of view, religions and spirituality are sources of the norms, ideals, and standards necessary for the survival of society, and therefore for the well-being of individual members of society. To the extent that a society's religions provide a sufficient degree of consensus on values, that particular society will be sufficiently strong to survive and persist through time. For example, Spain has widely shared religious and secular values that have perpetuated traditional families for long periods of time.

In the earliest stages of evolution, religions are relatively homogeneous groups —like Australian aboriginal tribes—whose participants are drawn from the whole of their communities (Durkheim, 1915). Because preliterate societies are smaller than today's modern industrialized societies, consensus in preliterate societies is easier to achieve and maintain (Hess, 1991). However, because there is very little distinction between individual and group identities in these societies, expressions of individual uniqueness are generally very difficult or impossible to achieve, so that creativity and innovation in preliterate societies are severely limited (Martin, 1990).

When societies evolve to become more differentiated and pluralistic, a certain degree of consensus of values is still necessary for social adaptation. It is often difficult for the United States to achieve consensus in light of its complex pluralism. Although religions may be divisive influences in some societies, rather than unifying forces, there must be some overall common denominators of interests and values for any society to adapt successfully. Evolution cannot occur, and a society will predictably become extinct, if this precondition of value consensus is not met (Ashbrook, 1993).

Because of this necessary interdependence, the quality of relationships maintained among religions in any given society is in the long-range interest of the society (Lenski, 1961; Yinger, 1957). There must be sufficient coordination and collaboration of shared interests that vital survival values and ideals, such as protection of the environment, are agreed upon by large groups of people. However scientific a community is, these prerequisites of social adaptation are nonetheless necessary, especially because secular values have not been able to replace religions satisfactorily in evolutionary processes (Macionis & Benokraitis, 1995).

RELIGION, MORAL AGENCY, AND SOCIAL CHANGE

Religion heightens awareness of capacities and responsibilities as moral agents (Blasi, 1991). People clarify and articulate their standards of right and wrong through their religious beliefs and practices, as well as select values they consider to be sacred or most precious. For example, Buddhism outlines distinctive, non-Western kinds of moral and family responsibilities, including a strong emphasis on a filial loyalty. Once people have established their priorities clearly, they can assume positions to allow for the exercise of their wills and energies as moral agents. Sometimes, however, morality may appear to conflict with religious priorities, and many moral and religious conflicts have been manifested and described as crises of conscience (McNamara, 1992). For example, religious believers may decide to be conscientious objectors in times of war instead of deciding that to go to war is the moral choice.

Religions increase meaning and purpose, and can subsequently establish effective directions and sufficiently motivated efforts to bring about social changes (Weber, 1958). Religions provide ideals for goals, which also bring fulfillment to individuals who deliberately act as moral agents. Becoming more complete as human beings focuses people's energies on making contributions to the whole of society (Schumaker, 1992).

One of the most powerful concepts in western religions is "God's will" (Ebaugh, 1993). If people believe that God has specific purposes or goals for them to accomplish, they also tend to believe that they can bring about these changes (Randour, 1993). Although interpretations of God's will are made with varying levels of commitment and enthusiasm, doing God's will can become a raison d'être, or a primary goal of day-to-day existence (Hussain, 1984).

RELIGION, MOTIVATION, AND SOCIAL CHANGE

Religions provide individuals with distinctive world views and specific assumptions about human nature (Strunk, 1979; Manuel & Manuel, 1979). People are motivated partly by their understanding of human nature, and partly by how they see themselves in the total scheme of things. They expect different things from themselves depending on their views about possibilities for human behavior and human relationships (McNamara, 1992).

Social changes occur predominantly in populations that have a certain degree of openness to new values (Ashbrook, 1993; Haney, 1989; Ryan, 1992). For example, where traditions such as obedience to hierarchical authority have infiltrated social organizations, modern values—which are frequently synonymous with secular values and which can sometimes reverse the priorities expressed by traditional values—may replace some of the rigidities of conventional social forms (Stark & Bainbridge, 1985). Similarly, members of groups must be open to ideas and realities related to changes before actual shifts can be realized (Martin, 1990). Therefore, in many respects religions may serve more as means, rather than ends, in the overall processes of social change (Roof, 1992).

Whether people are individually or collectively motivated by religions, they are more effective in accomplishing changes when their ideals, values, and goals are shared by the individuals and groups they care for most others or by those in power. For example, religions can legitimate changing the legal system or political procedures. Furthermore, changes grounded in religious values are more likely to be accepted by populations at large, thereby increasing their long-term effectiveness. People can accomplish more when they act collectively, and their shared religious or secular beliefs and values can be both sources of increased motivation and rationales for carrying actions to better degrees of resolution and fulfillment (Smith, 1991).

RELIGION, IDENTITY, AND SOCIAL CHANGE

In considering the relationship between religion, identity, and social change, it can be hypothesized that religions can either empower or disempower individuals and groups. Therefore it can be surmised that identity is not automatically strengthened in individuals who turn to religions as sources of their values. Thus, to meet individual needs as well as to accomplish constructive social changes in society, identifications with religious values must be highly selective; it is only creative and constructive ideals that promote social progress in the long run, such as respect for family responsibilities and egalitarian social structures.

To the extent that individuals choose to sustain the status quo rather than bring about change, they necessarily internalize traditional religious values rather than modern or innovative values. Such people frequently resist modifications of the status quo through their actions, and their daily activities become ritual-ized. It is only through individuals' deliberate choices to honor their own uniqueness, as well as their visions of a better society, that they can create innovative, constructive changes in society at large.

Qualitative social changes result from individual and collective activities in which people are engaged as meaningful social actors. This kind of socially effective behavior flows from identities that are more or less deliberately cre-ated and expressed. For example, when people such as leaders of political par-ties believe that they are powerful historical actors, they predictably increase their possibilities of being able to express this belief through their actions (Wil-son, 1986). Social changes in the direction of progress cannot occur through behavior that is not intentioned in some way (Appleyard, 1993), and it is only at best that society evolves in ways to fulfill human potentials rather than repress and suppress creative possibilities (Ashbrook, 1993).

QUESTIONS AND ANSWERS

Two questions help to assess some of the many complexities of social change processes: "To what extent and under which circumstances do religions promote social change?" and "To what extent and under which circumstances do reli-gions retard or inhibit social change?" Answers to these questions clarify the view of religious and secular dynamics in society, as well as their impact on the quality of life of members of different populations and cultures.

Only by using broad historical perspectives can people understand the depth and scope of denominational and sectarian influences on social structures and processes. For example, religious denominations, because they are closer to mainstream social values, tend to sustain the status quo more readily than reli-gious sects, whereas religious sects have a more innovative impact on existing social institutions.

Another important question to be asked is "What intensifies religious differ-ences so much that they lead to violence and wars?" To the extent that some of the negative consequences of closed belief systems can be documented and understood more fully, some of these group and societal clashes of interests may be prevented or neutralized. For example, although dogma and bigotry are individually and socially harmful, and thrive in the ossified authoritarian struc-tures of closed relationship systems, education can effectively modify these per-sonal, social, and structural closures.

Two additional questions to ask in assessing the role of religions in a broad sweep of history are: "To what extent is it important for people to identify themselves as members of the human race, rather than as members of particular religions?" and "Can particularized memberships in religious communities block people's ability to see more universalist aspects of themselves as members of the human race?" Although intrinsic tensions between the particular and the universal cannot be resolved, the broader picture of society, universal needs, and basic human responsibilities should be acknowledged by people developing specific religious allegiances and loyalties. Furthermore, although people inevitably have special preferences and responsibilities that relate to their different subcultures, in the long run they are responsible for achieving an acceptable level of general well-being in the world at large. Therefore, whatever their religious beliefs may be, individuals are participants in the community of nations rather than merely members of nation states.

GENERALIZATIONS

Because religions either precipitate or retard social changes, individual members of religions essentially make choices about the extent to which they precipitate or retard change. However, people are also integral parts of broad cultural patterns that themselves may simultaneously move toward or away from change.

Social class memberships have additional effects on individual and group abilities to speed up or slow down change processes. Being a member of a social class that has low status and little power is generally synonymous with having minimal influence over any kind of changes (Bendroth, 1994).

Extreme religious differences can generate volatile and pernicious social consequences (Goode, 1968). When there is marked disagreement among varied religions' cherished beliefs and values, their contradictory world views and discrepant behavior patterns may result in violent disputes or wars. Religions' potential for destruction must be acknowledged, especially because there is empirical documentation of the fact that some of the most gruesome crimes, as well as some of the most sublime acts, have been undertaken in the name of religions (Eisler, 1987).

However, when the broadest historical perspectives are applied to these phenomena, some of the conflicts generated by religious differences can be thought of as eventually bringing about constructive structural and political changes (Ashbrook, 1933). Furthermore, it is essentially the pervasiveness of overly rigid social structures—in society and in religious organizations—that creates the kinds of impassible, unbridgeable differences and contradictions that lead to war (Cornwall, 1987). Therefore, wherever belief and communication systems are

closed, social mechanisms need to be created as safety valves to prevent conflicts from escalating unnecessarily and becoming explosive.

PROPOSITIONS

The repeated rituals of traditional, denominational religions tend to ossify their
organizational structures through time, so that violent changes are more likely to
develop. By contrast, and more benignly, where religions have more flexible
organizational structures, less dramatic modifications of social forms and processes occur.

Religions may empower groups and individuals to work together to accomplish constructive social changes through strengthening their visions of alternative realities. Ideally, religions provide their believers with viable possibilities
for new social forms and processes, so that adaptations bring about improvements and progress (Manuel & Manuel, 1979; Smith, 1991). However, even
where religions have closed social systems that precipitate conflicts, it is possible to reverse these negative consequences and move toward constructive social changes, because individuals and groups have ever-present opportunities to
make new value choices to increase life-enhancing conditions.

Religions also endorse individual senses of belonging to the human race
through ritualization of shared life passages and regular celebrations of seasonal
and historical events. The passage of individual and social time is sanctified in
these ways, which both mark changes and denote particular time periods. Developing religious festivities around life stages, seasons, and sacralized events
allows people to observe and experience social changes that can occur whether
or not they want them.

The orthodoxy and potential orthodoxy of many religious beliefs can be
substantially modified through individualized prayer and meditation. The effect
of dogma is lessened by doing things differently, which opens up closed belief
systems. Refusing to obey traditional dictates also has the effect of opening up
closed belief systems. Thus individual and social freedom are increased through
individuals' strengthening their abilities to interpret and reinterpret religious
meanings, and through their relating these meanings to identity choices.

CHOICES

As in all parts of life, there are infinite choices for perceiving and responding to
religious and social changes. For example, people may decide to be part of such

changes or resolve to impede them. They may also decide to participate fully in the available varieties of religious worship or to be more peripheral in their participation and observances (Marty & Appleby, 1991). Another choice is either to follow religious dictates closely or to use inventiveness in interpreting religious traditions. In the latter instance, spiritual responses to conventional forms and processes are enhanced.

Choosing to avert problems resulting from extreme, irreconcilable differences in religious beliefs frequently includes choosing to work toward developing a more eclectic, ecumenical understanding among religious and spiritual groups. People tend either to raise their families to cherish traditions, thereby resisting modern innovations, or to work toward actively opening up religious and social systems, with the result that they can sustain more flexible relationships and transactions with others.

People must also make choices about the values and identities they honor. For example, they must decide whether to put their loyalties to particular religious communities above their membership in the whole human race. They also have to choose whether to accept or to reject others, and whether to tolerate or genuinely cherish the many differences that exist among people.

The larger picture of individuals and society must be taken seriously in choosing to participate in social changes. Members of nation states can only claim their full rights in the world community when they honor diversity among human beings by choosing more expansive world views as well as more inclusive values. Also, whatever the historical and social circumstances, choosing to be spiritual beings is predictably advantageous for those who want to grow and develop their potentials (Ashbrook, 1993). The case that follows explores one couple's success in developing a lifestyle in a new country, which called for both social change and the preservation of their heritage.

CASE STUDY

Sanje Veel was a 33-year old Indian man who had immigrated to the United States several years earlier to take a specialist professional position as a chemical engineer.

Sanje had brought Nene, his wife, with him, and they had both left their extended families in Bombay. Sanje and Nene were Hindus, although this had been more of an ethnic association over the years than an active religious faith.

The move to the United States had been the beginning of a new life for Sanje and Nene. However, it was stressful for both of them to overcome their initial culture shock and settle into a new lifestyle. In fact, it took several years for both Sanje and Nene to begin to feel at home in the United States, and even then Nene was very homesick for her family in India. As a result, their marriage was increasingly stressed by their isolation in a relatively alien American culture.

Sanje and Nene started family therapy to relieve the tensions and conflicts in their marriage. After a few months of clinical sessions, Nene decided to start a small business in Indian crafts. This decision led her to make many contacts with artisans in Bombay, and after a year she started to travel to India regularly for business purposes. During these trips Nene was able to reestablish contact with many members of her family.

Although Sanje did not accompany Nene during these visits to India, his own professional development went well in the United States, and he earned enough money to move their home from the suburbs to the city. This move gave Sanje and Nene more access to their cosmopolitan friends, which included increased numbers of Indian acquaintances made since coming to the United States. These community supports made Sanje and Nene less dependent on each other for a meaningful social life, and their relationship became more calm.

Analysis

Sanje and Nene were able to establish a more comfortable marriage through clinical intervention because they were able to see how to activate new dependencies that went beyond their own relationship. That is, Nene's new business with Indian contacts gave her a strong interest outside her marriage, which also effectively served to stabilize that relationship. Similarly, Sanje's professional success and their move to the city gave him sufficiently exciting preoccupations that he and Nene no longer looked only to each other to satisfy their emotional and cultural needs.

Sanje and Nene also drew on their Hindu heritage to broaden their world views and to find additional meaning in their everyday behavior. Nene tried to educate herself more about Hinduism to become more knowledgeable about Indian crafts and history. Sanje became more interested in Hinduism as he pursued Indian and American professional contacts, and made more friends with Indians also living in the area. Thus Hinduism gave both Sanje and Nene broader outlooks on life, and consequently they were able to be more philosophical about their interpersonal differences. Also, this kind of historical depth and connectedness to their own culture rooted their new life in the contrasting cultural setting. They began to believe they were part of a significant cultural exchange between East and West, and this feeling helped them to find new bearings in their more mundane activities.

The family contacts Nene made through her business travel were particularly helpful in giving her emotional as well as cultural independence. She was also able to step outside her family's traditional gender expectations for herself as she returned to the United States and made a success of the Indian crafts retail store she had opened. She felt freer in many significant ways as she proceeded in this direction of making a finely tuned individual contribution to the world of commerce.

STRATEGIES FOR CLINICAL INTERVENTIONS

Effective clinicians need clarity about their understanding and views of society, as well as about their understanding and views of interpersonal dynamics (Glassner & Freedman, 1979). Ideally, they should know what it means to be members of families or specific gender groups in this country at this particular time in history if they are to serve their clients well as effective change agents. Clinicians should also be aware of how changing secular or cultural values are reflected in religions and other social institutions.

The role of the responsible clinician ultimately demands that clinicians ask their clients to look at the world about them and assess its meanings selectively for themselves. This process is necessary because clinicians and clients alike are socialized to participate in broad social changes, whether or not they want to do so. It is only by orienting themselves to both small and large group contexts that clinicians can practice as meaningfully and as effectively as possible.

Therefore, the give and take of clinical exchanges benefits from including references to larger worlds outside the clinical setting, and ideally even to a universe outside that of the national society shared by clinician and client. For example, some clients can benefit from being asked what it means to be inhabitants of this planet, and what can be learned from history that is pertinent to their own individual and social concerns today and in the future. Clinicians are in strategic positions to help clients to build meaningful world views, and to assume roles as historical actors in these times of rapid and frequently disorienting change (Schumaker, 1992).

In these ways, clinical strategies metaphorically water the social and cultural roots of clients, as well as help them to create viable individual and social visions of the future (Haney, 1989). These strategies work beneficially because clients cannot be fully human or develop spiritually unless they can begin to honor both the details and the scope of their life chance possibilities. Even though both clinicians and clients may have deeply held religious beliefs, they must find responsible ways to bring these values to fruition by applying them to everyday situations and activities. Clinicians can effectively encourage and support clients' healthy quests to realize potential new worlds.

Thus, clinicians are agents of change within the contexts of both individual lives and societies. Improving relationships opens up family and social systems, so that more widespread impacts of individual modifications and adaptations can be experienced. Also, as clients realize their missions as historical actors in society, they become leaders of collective efforts to improve society beyond the immediate urgencies of particular problem-solving processes.

10 Clinical Tasks

1. Suggest to clients that they are historical actors, and trace the implications of this view.
2. Discuss clients' understanding of social change and their relationships to specific social change processes.
3. Challenge the assumptions clients make about change and human nature, and suggest ways to broaden and deepen their understanding.
4. Describe ways in which individual and social innovations are met with resistance from others.
5. Encourage clients to persist in seeing themselves in the broadest social, historical, and evolutionary contexts possible, especially when formulating their long-range goals.
6. Ask clients to describe what they believe are the most significant aspects of the personal histories of their own religious beliefs.
7. As clients to bridge their personal life histories with their knowledge of broad social and cultural changes.
8. Encourage clients to move toward changing social structures rather than becoming their victims.
9. Introduce and reinforce the concept that clients are necessarily agents of change.
10. Discuss the theme of individual moral agency in the context of broad change processes.

Chapter 11

Identity and Religion

Identities are strongly influenced by beliefs, and likewise beliefs, however secular, are markedly affected by religions and religious traditions. It is necessary for people to make decisions and commitments because they are moral agents; and they need to cope successfully with many individual and social limitations to survive. Myriad moral decisions and empirical assessments are required for people merely to conduct day-to-day business, whether they be members of a corporation or nurses.

Deep convictions and commitments frequently derive directly or indirectly from conventional religious denominations or sects (Stark & Glock, 1968). Perhaps surprisingly, people usually keep their religions throughout their lifetimes, and seldom deliberately convert to other religious traditions (Malony & Southard, 1992). Moreover, most people adapt their religious beliefs to their lifestyle needs, rather than make religion or religious values the cornerstone of their major or minor decision making. For example, going to a place of worship may be a social outing rather than a significant means of spiritual refreshment.

Seeing connections between specific beliefs and patterns of behavior frees people to cultivate identifications with those beliefs that hold the most meaning and potential fulfillment for them. This is a rewarding enterprise, because behavior flows from identities that are either achieved or imposed by others. To a large extent, people are who they think they are, especially when they unquestioningly accept others' views. In a similar way, if a child is viewed as a behavior problem, this opinion frequently becomes a self-fulfilling prophecy.

Examining and working out relationships between identities and religions or sacred beliefs are beneficial activities that can have far-reaching consequences. This is the way people decide, for example, whether they are divine beings or creatures of original sin. Furthermore, taking these tasks seriously allows people to be more true to themselves, as well as to make more social contributions.

PERSONAL CONTEXTS

Religion and identity are initially developed, and first linked in intellectual theorizing about behavior, through the emotionally significant interpersonal context of families (Fromm, 1967). People learn about religions, as well as practice them, largely because of the dominance or influence of emotionally significant others (Bowen, 1978). Furthermore, the impact of these beliefs and practices may remain essentially indelible for a lifetime (Johnson, 1973).

Identities are net balances of personal and others' views of individual moral agencies. When people allow others to define them more strongly than they define themselves, they are necessarily inadequate in their personal and public communications (Barker, 1984). However, when people define their identities meaningfully, decisively, and consistently, they become effective moral agents (Hall, 1991).

Thus, although identities and religions are powerful determinants of individual and social behavior, it is when people examine how they relate to particular members of their families that they may understand more fully who they are and who they want to be. Family dependencies historically dictate which religious beliefs are internalized. Furthermore, making decisions about identities and beliefs in relation to significant others is a crucial stage of strengthening both personal and public behavior (Bendroth, 1994).

Therefore, attention should be paid not only to personal domains and public performances if lasting contributions to society are to be made. Both cherished personal beliefs and the social sources of those beliefs must be honored so as to attain either individual or social goals. Religious values permeate everyday realities, and individual well-being is inextricably related to societal progress (Berger & Luckmann, 1967). Individuals are both personal and social in their most fulfilling modes of behavior.

To thrive as well as possible, individuals must nurture their identities in solitude and silence at least some of the time. This is why it is important to create safe places for prayer, meditation, contemplation, and reflection; that is, to construct situations where this vital work can take place without interruption. For example, weekend retreats or quiet evening pastimes may be vital to maintaining spiritual and emotional balance. Thus making a commitment to lead a reflective life ultimately expedites establishing direct associations between identity and religion. Because these tasks are never completely accomplished, efforts to find and cherish solitude must be sustained for people to continue to live more fully.

WORK SYSTEMS

Even though work systems may seem far removed from issues of identity and religion, most people end up with the particular kinds of work they do because of the interplay between their identities and religions or other belief systems. For example, teachers may believe that they are passing on the word of God, or the truth, to new members of society, thus creating future well-being for all. Efforts to find occupations for which affinity is truly felt are most successful when strong identities, based on internalized, genuine values and beliefs, discern projects that really "fit" individual needs for meaning. For example, people who become doctors believe that medicine is the right profession in which to make their contribution to society.

Thus, ideally religions—and more particularly prayer, meditation, or contemplation rather than ritual—frequently orient people to choose vocations that seem to suit them. Both religious and secular vocations optimally synthesize unique skills and interests with shared concerns, so that specific work trajectories or career paths can be followed by individuals to give the most possible to society.

Work systems deserve close scrutiny, because it is in these milieus that the most formal, and perhaps the most long-lasting, contributions to society are made. The extent to which potentials are expressed can be discerned by examining individuals' functioning in relation to others in the same work systems. Consideration must also be given to whether contributions are recognized and respected, and whether creative innovations are welcomed. Analyzing autonomous uses of time, and whether workers are required to follow directions or do busy work, is also an enlightening enterprise. People need to do what they believe in if they are to find their work rewarding.

When it is difficult to align beliefs and identities through examining patterns of interaction in families, seeing the self in work systems is particularly advantageous. For example, because individuals are less involved in their work than in their families, and because work systems are less intense than family emotional systems, it is often easier to analyze the dynamics of a work system than those of a family system. Because values and beliefs are inescapable, they are expressed in all occupational exchanges. Thus work systems, in addition to families, become prisms for understanding behavior and identifying ultimate concerns, as well as for assessing the effectiveness of personal talents and skills.

POLITICAL ORGANIZATION

Power in society is most easily observed by examining formal and informal political organization, that is, political institutions and the innumerable interpersonal and interest group alliances that underlie those same institutions and their cultures. Examples of these alliances are environmental agencies and organizations that represent the interests of unemployed people. Historically and traditionally, political organization has been hierarchical and characterized by patterns of dominance and authority derived from the statuses and resources of mainstream interest groups.

Identity and religion can have substantial impacts on these traditional power structures and political institutions, because the mutuality of identity and religion may be an effective catalyst in precipitating changes in political organization (Yinger, 1957). Power structures result from repeated processes and routinized patterns of behavior, which, although frequently ritualized, are not predetermined; therefore, to some extent individual or collective strategies may break through even the most resistant political structures and institutions. For example, the civil rights movement was able to reduce some discriminatory practices in housing practices and in the workforce.

Because identity and religion can provide meaning and direction for work, they can also define vocations for participation in political organization. Thus clarifying values and strengthening identities create ways out of political apathy, political entanglements, and political contradictions. These achievements are possible because people have the capacity to neutralize power and its diverse political manifestations when their actions are securely anchored in their individual and social identities.

Just as religions comprise distinctive belief systems, political organization is driven by specific beliefs about power, goals, and ideals. Furthermore, although political organization may seem to be immutable, strong identities can initiate and influence long-term political changes. Some prime ministers and presidents, for example, have initiated legislative or policy changes that consequently lasted for many years.

IDENTITY, RELIGION, AND HISTORY

Identity and religion are inextricably related to each other, as well as to society and history. In fact, identities are only fully understood when they are put into historical contexts, and when individual behavior and patterns of interaction are viewed as being expressed by historical actors. All people are products of their immediate historical circumstances. Thus identity, religion, and history link individuals to both intimate relationships and values, as well as to broad social trends and influences.

Human beings are at the same time unique and integral parts of social currents. Their identities are the most effective means through which their individual and social values can be consolidated and prioritized, so that energies are sufficiently harnessed for effective accomplishments (Van Zandt, 1991). The realization that values and actions have significant social influences, and that therefore individuals have inevitable impacts on history, can strengthen identities and makes actions more goal-directed. Some scientific discoveries, for example, have been dictated by the necessities of historical conditions. These processes are particularly evident in the contributions of charismatic religious leaders such as Saint Paul (Blasi, 1991).

Thus religions serve as bridges that link individuals to history. Through choosing to express specific values, people anchor themselves in social institutions, which move slowly and according to the ebb and flow of history. However, although individuals have choices about the values with which they identify, they do not have choices about whether to define their identities or to participate in history. If people do not opt to construct their own identities, others inevitably do it for them. Also, they are inevitably historical actors whether or not they acknowledge this fact. Furthermore, their experiences of subjective well-being depend on the nature of their social or religious involvement, mutuality, and reciprocity (Ellison, 1991).

INDIVIDUALITY AND THE UNIVERSE

Each person's uniqueness has an impact on the universe at large. Human beings are relatively minuscule, but mathematically they count for something, so that the mental and physical consequences of their merely being alive change the nature of their immediate environments as well as the universe. By examining their identities and values through the lenses of religions, humans discover their uniqueness, as well as ways to express this sacred uniqueness in the universe.

Identity and religion link individuals with the broadest realities and visions of human existence (Mol, 1978). People learn that the nation state and the world system have permeable boundaries, and that the depth and breadth of their experiences are ultimately unfathomable (Kaufman, 1993). However, consciousness gives individuals freedom to select from many possibilities, and it is by cultivating awareness of some of the necessary identifications with the universe that humans can best develop their potentials. For example, awareness is heightened through a variety of prayer modes as well as through meditation and contemplation (Poloma & Gallup, 1991).

States of being result from degrees of understanding about the universe and human nature, and from decisions made about using talents. These postures influence individual abilities to become effective historical actors and moral agents through their everyday behavior (Hall, 1990a). Furthermore, self-knowledge leads to individual and social betterment, as well as to true concern for societal well-being, rather than merely to personal gratification.

Thus both the height and depth of being are expressed through identities, which are built on a daily basis. However, some people may discover their true identities more easily than others, especially in times of crisis, or because their most satisfying modes of individual and social being are consistently close to what they actually do each day.

VOCATION

In addition to articulating and consolidating identities through value choices, individuals need clear-mindedness to fully experience and respond to a void. That is, being open- rather than closed-minded allows for the achievement of humans' fullest potentials, as well as for the recognition and emulation of inspired guidance or enlightenment (Hunsberger, 1985).

Historically and traditionally, in Western civilizations this posture of openness has been described as listening to the word of God, or waiting to discern the will of God. However, intellectually conceptualizing this condition of readiness is necessarily significantly less important than making actual efforts to achieve it. In fact, people cannot accomplish great deeds or ideals if their minds are unnecessarily cluttered with their own or others' unproductive ideas. Inspiration and opportunities must be seized when they appear, especially because it is through these kinds of symbolic communications with the universe that religious or secular vocations are formulated and realized.

Although "vocation" literally means "a calling," a vocation can be thought of as a particular kind of awareness that appears to originate in either external or internal supernatural or divine sources. However, to be able to hear any calling, a person must have a listening or waiting readiness for a voice or voices. Thus, some degree of expectancy in attitude must be maintained, whatever activities are undertaken. Furthermore, people need deliberately to heighten their awareness of the contents of their minds for the express purpose of recognizing any callings. For example, it is not possible to receive a vocation to pursue a particular program in higher education unless there is some degree of readiness to hear that communication.

Vocations are meaningful in that people are more likely to be in a state of grace, or perfect harmony, if they recognize and follow their vocations. Deliberate alignments of daily tasks with the ineffable generally spell out specific steps to be taken for the realization of vocations (Poloma & Gallup, 1991). It is thus that vocations are frequently revealed a little at a time rather than in one spiritual event (Randour, 1993).

IDENTITY

An individual's tasks to forge identity are necessarily unfinished at death. Thus this particular challenge outlasts all other challenges, because self-discovery and self-realization remain as important goals even at the time of death, and through the experience of death.

Identities are not physiologically limited by skins, and human imagination can touch the outer shores of the universe when identities are built on the deepest values and most basic human beliefs. Although there are many environmental and biological determinants of existence, such as hereditary health conditions, human beings are not in and of themselves confined by physical parameters in their thoughts. Even though ultimately psychological and physical well-being are preeminent, the most satisfying lives are usually built on purpose and meaning (James, 1969; Tillich, 1952). Thus religions can be used as means, as well as being ends in themselves, and true membership in religious communities is realized by practicing their values as identities. This principle is particularly clear in the case of conversions, where overlaps between individual and community beliefs are both more visible and more psychically apparent (Rambo, 1993).

Identity is the core of being, and being is the core of existence and survival (Tillich, 1952). Being conscious means experiencing awareness of the "I am" in identities, as well as awareness of being led or of being a historical actor (Mol, 1978). Personal interaction needs to be balanced with the smallest and largest groups that make up social dependency. In fact, people can only be truly independent and autonomous when they accept their universal, even sacred interdependency (Hall, 1986b). Such relationships are symbolized as sacred communities within many religious systems.

QUESTIONS AND ANSWERS

Realistic questions to ask in any appraisal of the relationship between identity and religion are "To what extent can people change the religions their families gave or did not give them when they were children?" and "Is it satisfactory merely to modify ascribed religious beliefs to increase meaning, or is it preferable to adopt new religions?"

One answer is that people should at least be prepared to change religions if necessary. However, in most instances religious denominations, if not religious sects, have sufficient flexibility within their varied belief systems so that substantial individual modifications can be made without dramatic conversions or substitutions. It is the very act of going in the direction of carving out meaning that reveals the deepest aspects of self, and the deepest connections between self and society.

Other issues that need more clarification include "How do solitude and silence enhance identity?" and "To what extent do prayer and meditation provide guidance, or even fulfillment, while strengthening identity?" These related questions suggest that the commitment to live a contemplative life is complex, and may or may not be beneficial. If people turn to religions to find increased meaning, purpose, and direction, traditional modes of communication with godheads—prayer, meditation, and contemplation—may clarify and enrich their everyday decision making. However, to experiment satisfactorily with these powerful mechanisms, it is essential to include solitude and silence in one's daily routine. Only by giving attention to these specific efforts to commune with supernatural powers can people experience sufficient or adequate returns. For example, achievements of mystical unity and grace essentially depend on giving these states a considerable degree of exclusive concentration.

GENERALIZATIONS

Because identities are strongly influenced by beliefs, an important fact to record in life histories is whether people's current religious beliefs derive from their families or from emotionally significant others. To strengthen identities, an assessment of which beliefs individuals authentically own must be made, as well as of which ones individuals automatically absorbed without realizing the inevitable negative consequences of creating contradictions and confusion among personal defining principles (Bowen, 1978).

Priorities in individuals' belief systems can be outlined by understanding the roles emotional dominance played in early religious or secular education, and to what extent it continues to permeate current beliefs. For example, how the most influential adults in individuals' childhoods defined the ways a particular religion was practiced needs to be examined, as well as whether these conventions are still observed, even though they may no longer be meaningful. In this situation benefits result both from discarding less vital beliefs and from clinging tenaciously to more cherished values.

A failure to construct one's identity actively means that others will inevitably do so as a consequence of one's passivity. In other words, unless uniqueness is discovered and deliberately expressed, it is lost. Furthermore, because others cannot fully know or appreciate an individual's uniqueness, individuals must necessarily honor it themselves through strengthening the integrity in their everyday decision making (McNamara, 1992).

Identifying with the universe can also help people to understand and develop their uniqueness (Butterworth, 1969). When they consciously live in the broadest arenas of life, they can understand more fully and more clearly how to make their finest contributions to society. Because the boundaries between the private and public spheres of people's lives are permeable, people can only be wholly human when they claim and give of their talents to others.

PROPOSITIONS

Identities influence beliefs, actions, and contributions to society strongly, but to a large extent people tend essentially to inherit the religions from which their beliefs, actions, and contributions derive. Therefore, it is more important to understand the complex accommodation processes of people's existing beliefs than dramatic shifts in beliefs like conversion, even though historically more conversions have occurred in modern than in traditional societies (Rambo, 1993).

Identifying with their own convictions helps people to withstand others' pressures to conform to community beliefs or to meet others' expectations. Ideally, they also recognize how their value choices about identity derive from complex socialization processes. When they are decisive about the substance of their identities, people essentially neutralize their more or less automatic inclinations merely to absorb and manifest the beliefs of those who are emotionally closest to them (Bowen, 1978). Therefore true independence exists only through people's making series of autonomous choices about which values and beliefs are personally authentic (Hall, 1990a).

The bases of values may not be readily located within particular national or international boundaries (Hechter et al., 1993). Furthermore, people become more spiritual or transcendent when they connect themselves with values from varied national and cultural settings (Kaufman, 1993). Thus selected values relate to the universe at large as well as to the immediacy of family cultures.

CHOICES

Understanding the social sources of values creates an advantageous position from which to realize individual connectedness with others. Because people cannot exist in vacuums, they isolate themselves only at their peril. By contrast, choosing to recognize the social sources of deep-seated beliefs becomes a liberating experience. Individuals formulate clearer senses of their identities, as well as find increased meaning, when they realize some of the ways in which they are linked to social institutions and social structures (Bendroth, 1994).

Religions have rich cultures of their own, as well as deep roots in time. By participating in religious rituals, people necessarily make contact with the past from which these religions developed (Beckford & Luckmann, 1989). Just as individuals cannot escape from the social sources of their identities, they also cannot take themselves out of history. Their value choices and their choices to participate in religions, albeit in a wide variety of ways, anchor them in basic social institutions (Malony & Southard, 1992).

Consolidating and periodically reexamining new knowledge about the self and others, rather than treating day-to-day facts and interactions superficially, is vital to individual and social well-being (Berger & Luckmann, 1967). Individuals honor reality most through their efforts to understand their value choices as fully as possible. Powerful empirical consequences result from these choices, and selected values and ideals soon become physical, emotional, and mental realities, as well as expressions of spiritual integrity (Blasi, 1991). Self-identification is explored in the next case study.

CASE STUDY

Nancy Chinn was a 26-year-old Vietnamese woman who had been adopted by an American couple when she was a small child. Originally, Nancy had come from a Buddhist family, but she had been brought up as an observant Protestant by her American family. She had two older American brothers and two older American sisters.

As an adolescent, Nancy had had more than the usual kinds of identity crises. She had tried to resolve some of her cultural and social insecurities by becoming very popular with boys, and she had married an American man at age 20. She had two small children, and sought clinical intervention for help with her conflictual marriage and her feelings of intense overresponsibility for the care of her children.

Nancy gained perspective on her current situation by examining the family dynamics of her American family and by doing some research about Vietnamese adoptees. She also tried to discover more about her Vietnamese cultural heritage, thus seeking to strengthen her identification with this national context and history.

During the course of therapy, Nancy's marriage became more manageable for her, but her husband continued to absent himself from child care responsibilities. Nancy began to realize that she had to meet her own emotional and intellectual needs, so she enrolled in a program in Asian studies at a local university. She found that this project was very rewarding, and she also joined an extracurricular Asian Club, which sponsored intellectual events about Asian culture, as well as provided group travel to Asia.

Analysis

Nancy was able to lessen the conflict in her marriage by defining her own identity more clearly. She was also able to cope more effectively with parenting by nurturing her own intellectual and cultural interests. Her research on her American family brought with it some needed detachment from those dependencies. As a youngest, culturally unique child in that system, as well as an adoptee, she had absorbed an uncomfortable amount of positive and negative attention and energy from other family members over the years. These patterns of dependency and interaction had resulted in her restricting her freedom to be her own self.

Nancy found that her increasingly empowered identity also gave her a variety of options for exploring her Asian heritage. She became particularly interested in Buddhism, which provided her with a new world view and a new philosophy of life. Before long, she felt less pressured to accomplish the kinds of material goals her parents had promoted through their characteristically Western and Christian ideals.

Nancy's focus on her cultural differences increased her emotional security and her sense of self-confidence. She became much more able to be a person in her own right with her parents, brothers, sisters, husband, and children than she had ever been able to be before. Therapy kept her focused on what was most important for her to accomplish at this time of crisis, and she was able to envision and follow through with plans that reconnected her to her cultural heritage and past. She realized that her education in these matters would take her more than a lifetime to accomplish; this realization left her with a heightened sense of satisfaction and the feeling that she needed to do much more work. She was no longer merely reactive to her husband and children, because her stronger identity essentially immunized her from being preoccupied with what others were doing, which had been the essence of her former concerns.

STRATEGIES FOR CLINICAL INTERVENTIONS

Clinicians are most effective when they both see and understand the many micro- and macrodimensions of their clients' identities. Because many clients' presenting problems are related to feelings of isolation and meaninglessness, as well as to their inner and external conflicts or contradictions, they can benefit a great deal from examining their value choices and strengthening their autonomy.

At more advanced stages of this learning process, increasing clients' senses of meaning and their motivation to contribute to others necessarily enhances their own well-being, purpose, and direction.

Clinical discussions should ideally cover both the breadth and depth of topics related to identity and religion (Randour, 1993). Great latitude needs to be given to clients at all times, however, so that they can clarify their own definitions, special interests, and preferences at all times. Thus the purpose of clinical questioning and confrontation largely becomes that of heightening clients' awareness of their value choices, of the value choices others make for them, and of the possibilities for making new value choices.

Establishing meaningful contact between clients and clinicians is an important way to establish and encourage clients' growth and maturation. This contact does not need to be very frequent, especially once clients' immediate presenting problems are sufficiently resolved, but some continuity in scheduling clinical meetings over long periods of time is highly recommended. For example, a regular sequence of monthly meetings for approximately a year is more likely to produce sound clinical results than a short period of very intensive meetings focused only on a quick, but perhaps not very satisfactory, resolution of specific presenting problems. Where clients are interested in accomplishing long-term results, or in taking preventive measures, they need to be advised early in the series of clinical exchanges that the complexity of learning required for understanding and making changes around value-laden, emotional issues cannot be achieved in a few weeks (Bowen, 1978).

This length of inquiry and the depth of research into the linkages between identity and religion are foundations for further refinements of clinical interventions. For example, a responsible definition of the self as a moral agent underlies the resolution of problematic relationships, substance abuse, domestic violence, and many other behavioral symptoms. Once a positive posture to everyday life is accomplished through empowering identity, clients can predictably at least cope effectively with their most difficult contingencies and situations, and in some cases their transcendence of negative conditions can bring about considerable individual achievements and contributions to society.

10 Clinical Tasks

  1. Ask clients to outline ways in which their identities are influenced by religions.

2. Examine how clients can use religious sources to empower their identities individually and socially.
3. Show how becoming more authentic through value choices can reestablish connections with religious beliefs and practices.
4. Discuss ways to increase autonomy through value choices and selected religious beliefs.
5. Outline definitions of vocation and how religious or secular callings can change purpose and direction in clients' lives.
6. Discuss knowledge about conversion processes, and how this knowledge can clarify the linkages between identity, religion, and social action.
7. Examine and discuss some of the political underpinnings of religious behavior and religious organizations.
8. Suggest ways in which clients can empower identities sufficiently to neutralize or minimize political influences in their lives.
9. Define ways in which aligning identities and religions or beliefs can lead to personal and social fulfillment.
10. Support clients in their quests to make more meaningful value choices in strengthening their identities.

Chapter 12

Conclusions

Examinations of substantive themes related to identity and religion inevitably lead to a variety of action consequences that are difficult to categorize clearly and meaningfully. People do not have the option of escaping the consequences of this knowledge, because it changes the ways in which reality is perceived and decisions are made. Everything people think and feel directs them to act; and, even when they do not want to act, their thoughts and feelings ultimately lead to their making different kinds of responses from those they made before acquiring this knowledge. Likewise, the development of scientific knowledge has a similar impact on individual and social behavior (Appleyard, 1993).

Religions are characterized by their own distinctive values and priorities. For example, the values of Protestantism and Judaism are often considered to be incompatible. However, it is some of the shared properties of religious experiences—for example, modalities of prayer and meditation—that may best guide expressions of the substance, and of the most creative or constructive aspects, of religious beliefs, rather than their distinctive characteristics. Also, being interested in and committed to religion in general, rather than being committed to a particular religion, may be of more assistance in reaching the heights of fulfillment than being interested in and committed to only one religion. People who are observant in their religious practices share much in common. In fact, believing in only one religion may encourage a rather dangerous development of overly narrow and dogmatic views of the world and others. Ideally, people need to remain open to new possibilities as individuals and as societies if they are to lead rich and rewarding lives (Butterworth, 1969).

One consequence of studying the relationships between identity and religion is that everyday experimentation with value choices increases. For example, people try one or another line of action to increase their individual or social fulfillment, and thus they come to understand the impact they can have on the quality of their lives as they make trial and error commitments to particular values through their actions. Over time, they can fairly easily assess the empirical consequences of, for instance, honoring the values of education or family relationships in their everyday behavior.

Thus individuals get clearer senses of the social sources of their identities and social contributions when they are willing and able to undertake such experiments. In similar ways, they can estimate some of the individual and social effects of choosing to express their energies for themselves or for others. They can actually observe how the quality of their lives changes, depending on the kinds of orientations they adopt toward themselves and others. Furthermore, clinical sociology is a professional discipline that provides meaningful frames of reference for such observations and assessments (Glassner & Freedman, 1979).

SOCIAL SOURCES OF IDENTITY

The more closely identity is examined, the more clearly the linkages between who people think they are and the social sources of those views can be seen. Religions continue to be significant social sources of identities, whether or not they are salient parts of individuals' lives. Thus religions have a social reality that needs to be reckoned with clinically as well as socially (Warner, 1993), and human consciousness remains very significant in moral development and even evolution (Teilhard de Chardin, 1965).

As well as knowing which influences shape identities, people must respond to others' images. For example, families have cultures or value systems in their own right, which may or may not embrace specific religious belief systems. Although individuals may not accept significant others' images and definitions, their social class memberships continue to be powerful ways of defining them. However, although social status frequently sets the scene for the quality and outcomes of many exchanges with others, ultimately it is definitions of self, rather than status or significant others' views, that can make real differences and have more predictable social consequences.

The cultures and societies in which people live are also sources of identities. People are who they are in part because of even the broadest social influences. Because individuals cannot survive in vacuums, they necessarily take on some of the characteristics of their immediate and remote environments. Thus cultural, social, and political trends both modify religions and directly affect identities. For example, being born in the same birth cohort of the U.S. baby boom can have specific social, cultural, and spiritual consequences (Roof, 1992).

SOCIAL CONSEQUENCES OF IDENTITY

A predictable linkage between identities and behavior is that people ultimately act in accordance with who they believe they are (Progoff, 1985). In fact, it is the substance and intensity of their identities that largely determine what they do with their lives (Hall, 1990a). A direct result of this association of identity with behavior is that changing identities has a more long-term effect on modifying behavior than changing only specific behaviors (Goffman, 1959).

If people are to become who they really want to be, they need to pay attention to their identities, rather than merely to specific goals or strategies (Tillich, 1952). If they want to change their lives, the most effective way to do so is to focus on the many different ways to change identities. Therefore, examining one's values, as well as scrutinizing one's religious and secular beliefs, is an effective and essential way to initiate desired modifications, in the same way that societies maintain collective searches for their souls through time (Jung, 1933).

Social consequences that flow from identities reach far beyond interpersonal concerns about religions or values. Even though people automatically interact from the bases of their identities, the more they understand these identities, the more they are able to take charge of their lives and make meaningful contributions to others.

It is valuable to use an evolutionary perspective when trying to understand the human spirit (Ashbrook, 1993). Social structures, social institutions, and evolution itself can be thought of as resulting in part from the behavioral consequences of collective identities. Thus, the future of Planet Earth may be intimately tied to the moral agency of human beings, which is the essence of identities (Teilhard de Chardin, 1965). With which religions people identify is not as significant as with which values they identify. Because of these consequences, individuals must necessarily be highly discriminating in determining their priorities. One thing to bear in mind is that trying to absorb an entire complex religious tradition, like that of Roman Catholicism, may be destructive to both personal and social well-being, in that such values can form unnecessarily rigid, relatively closed belief systems.

RELIGION AND PRIORITIES

One conclusion that can be drawn, at least tentatively, from examining identity and religion is that religions characteristically establish hierarchies among avail-

able values and ideals. The historical contexts and ritualistic emphases of religions are indicators of what it is that particular religious traditions value most.
Furthermore, it is these very priorities that can guide people in their choices
of what to honor in their own lives, which can help to clarify the need to
make decisions that eventually achieve or maintain mental health (Schumaker,
1992).

Although traditionally some religions are more otherworldly than others, many
contemporary values can be derived from religious sources (Kaufman, 1993).
To distinguish between the sacred and the profane, or between what is acceptable and what is unacceptable, religious belief systems implicitly rank their
values, with some values having greater moral worth than others (Durkheim,
1915). Thus cosmologies become comprehensive belief systems, which can be
used as resources in clinical interventions (Hall, 1986b). Even though it is important to get beyond hierarchical thinking for mental health purposes (Chopp,
1989), as well as to transcend clearly demarcated social orders (Smith, 1987),
the necessity for making choices calls forth skills to distinguish constructive
values accurately from destructive.

Another priority among some but not all religions is the emphasis placed on
the importance of having and expressing a direct faith in supernatural powers. If
people believe that the best will happen to them, this belief cultivates distinctive
modes of valuing unseen and unknown individual and social phenomena. For
example, having a deep positive faith in God engenders trust in a constructive
rather than a destructive future, where all people will be able to meet their real
needs and express their true interests.

An overall advantage of turning to religions to establish priorities is that
religions have effectively guided human beings through time amidst their many
complex wanderings (Lenski, 1961; Yinger, 1957). Furthermore, when people
get in touch with their deepest beliefs, they are more able to define what they
want to accomplish and where they want to go (Fromm, 1967).

ORIENTATION

People only know where they are going when they can articulate their own
perspectives (Strunk, 1979). Examining identity and religion gives them a sense
of who they are, and what their starting points and goals are (Schumaker, 1992).
Thus orientations serve them for the present second, the next few minutes, a
day, week, year, or decade (James, 1969).

To the extent that religions characteristically embrace timeless values, people
can transcend existing harsh realities by incorporating this kind of long-range

inspiration into their daily living patterns (Pollner, 1989). Seeing the broader picture and putting lives in perspective become possible for individuals by turning to religious beliefs as resources and contexts for actions (Berger & Luckmann, 1967).

Orientation creates a particular tilt or slant on life, which influences activity in certain directions (Progoff, 1985). Furthermore, even apparently slight differences have marked impacts on individuals' directions and purposes (Bowen, 1978). Thus even though orientation may appear to be relatively insignificant, it defines quality of life in profound ways (Kaufman, 1993).

Identity and religion are themselves powerful sources of orientation. In comparison with other kinds of orientations—such as levels of educational accomplishment or political affiliations—identity and religion appear to have some of the most far-reaching behavioral consequences for individuals, communities, and societies (Smith, 1991). Thus identity and religion are both interpersonal and broad social influences, which need to be expressed in decision making and actions for individuals to lead balanced and morally rich lives (Cornwall, 1987).

GIVING TO SELF

One way to become empowered is to take oneself seriously and to move toward the ideals that are cherished most (Hall, 1990a). Denying individual being and values is ultimately self-destructive, and restricts opportunities to develop the highest good (James, 1969). Such disempowerment makes it impossible to give to oneself or others (Hall, 1990b).

Paradoxically, when people are oriented toward giving to sufficient numbers of others, they can also give to themselves. For example, making contributions to communities can be a person's highest good, and by focusing on others' needs the person simultaneously satisfies his or her most intimate individual yearnings for meaning and purpose. Interacting in broad communities increases emotional security while at the same time increasing opportunities for fulfillment (Durkheim, 1951). This outcome results in large part from a person's consistently making value choices that reflect socially recognized priorities (Collins, 1990).

Giving to the self includes taking care of essential individual physical, mental, emotional, and spiritual needs. Becoming strong in all these areas results in being more resourceful and more able to contribute to others (Hall, 1986a). Ideally, such empowerment processes should precede individuals' attempts to give to others, because if social giving is done prematurely, these efforts may backfire as well as yield ineffective or negative results.

GIVING TO OTHERS

If giving to others is to benefit all, this giving needs to be authentic and heart-felt. Ideally, contributions should be synchronized with identities, which are themselves based on selected beliefs and values. Furthermore, when identities include some religious values, giving to others may be an outgrowth of this orientation.

Giving to others is influenced by empirical conditions and consequences as well as moral considerations. A strengthened identity necessarily includes behaving in life-enhancing ways. Once individual needs have been met, others' needs are automatically considered and met whenever possible.

There are many ways in which clinicians can help their clients to formulate meaningful and effective orientations, the most significant being to enable them to make value choices that are true to their own priorities and identities. This task may include orienting clients toward religious values, from which they select the values they find most significant; or giving to clients may be little more than getting out of their way, so that they may make their own choices. However, whatever strategy clinicians adopt, they must allow clients to be themselves, rather than block their inclinations and accomplishments (Hall, 1990a). Ideally clinicians encourage clients to value who they really are in all circumstances.

For clinicians, clients, and others, if they want to be strong as individuals in their own right, it is imperative that ultimately they give directly to others. This is so because people actually help themselves through their own acts of compassion (Wuthnow, 1991), and they can only maintain their own strength if they give to others. Giving to others is therefore a primary and essential way to give to the self, and personal well-being is inextricably tied to the well-being of others (Wuthnow, 1991).

FULFILLMENT

Substantive issues that concern identity and religion provide evidence demonstrating that people are interdependent, in that their true individual fulfillment is based on their abilities to make social contributions to bring about increased social fulfillment (Schumaker, 1992). To the extent that religions signal possible directions for individual and social fulfillment (Hall, 1986b), these orientations bring their own rewards and move individuals in directions of societal progress (Jung, 1933). Because identity empowerment provides sufficient motivation to transcend individual and social limitations, being fulfilled becomes a real possibility (Hall, 1990b).

Examinations of identity and religion in families, social classes, culture, and society show that fulfillment can also be assessed and achieved in these contexts. Restoring balance in individual lives, and in society at large, through participating constructively in these social institutions is a necessary but not a sufficient precondition for fulfillment.

Gender differences also indicate ways in which religions can empower people and move them toward fulfillment (Chopp, 1989). Although perhaps it is more realistic to think of achievements as merely moving toward fulfillment, rather than actually achieving it, great contrasts can be experienced between activities that go toward fulfillment and those that go toward self-destruction (Appleyard, 1993). Also, people perhaps gain more satisfaction by moving in a particular direction rather than by achieving specific finite goals (Hunsberger, 1985).

Identity and religion are vital centers or guides. They respond to basic human needs that crave to be fulfilled, so that strengthening identities through incorporating religious values increases both individual and social fulfillment. Individual well-being can ultimately derive only from community or social well-being, and fulfillment results from both individual and social realities (Wuthnow, 1991).

REFERENCES

Appleyard, B. (1993). *Understanding the present: Science and the soul of modern man.* New York: Doubleday.

Ashbrook, J. B. (Ed.). (1993). *Brain, culture, and the human spirit: Essays from an emergent evolutionary perspective.* Lanham, MD: University Press of America.

Barker, E. (1984). *The making of a Moonie: Brainwashing or choice.* Oxford, U.K.: Basil Blackwell.

Beckford, J. A., & Luckmann, T. (Eds.). (1989). *The changing face of religion.* Newbury Park, CA: Sage.

Bendroth, M. L. (1994). *Fundamentalism and gender: 1875 to the present.* New Haven, CT: Yale University Press.

Berger, P. L., & Luckmann, T. (1967). *The social construction of reality.* Garden City, NY: Doubleday.

Blasi, A. J. (1991). *Making charisma: The social construction of Paul's public image.* New Brunswick, NJ: Transaction.

Bowen, M. (1978). *Family therapy in clinical practice.* New York: Aronson.

Butterworth, E. (1969). *Unity of all life.* New York: Harper and Row.

Chopp, R. S. (1989). *The power to speak: Feminism, language, God.* New York: Cross-road.

Clark, E. J. (1990). The development of contemporary clinical sociology. *Clinical Sociology Review, 8,* 100–115.

Collins, P. H. (1990). *Black feminist thought: Knowledge, consciousness, and the politics of empowerment.* Boston: Unwin Hyman.

Cooley, C. H. (1964). *Human nature and the social order.* New York: Schocken.

Cornwall, M. (1987). The social bases of religion: A study of the factors influencing religious beliefs and commitment. *Review of Religious Research, 29,* 44–56.

Daly, M. (1968). *The church and the second sex.* Boston: Beacon Press.

Durkheim, E. (1915). *The elementary forms of the religious life.* New York: Free Press.

Durkheim, E. (1951). *Suicide.* Glencoe, IL: Free Press.

Ebaugh, H. R. (1993). *Women in the vanishing cloister: Organizational decline in Catholic religious orders in the United States.* New Brunswick, NJ: Rutgers University Press.

Eisler, R. (1987). *The chalice and the blade: Our history, our future.* San Francisco: Harper & Row.

Ellison, C. G. (1991). Religious involvement and subjective well–being. *Journal of Health and Social Behavior, 32,* 80–99.

Erickson, V. L. (1993). *Where silence speaks: Feminism, social theory and religion.* Minneapolis, MN: Fortress Press.

Finke, R., & Stark, R. (1992). *The churching of America, 1776–1990*. New Brunswick, NJ: Rutgers University Press.

Fromm, E. (1967). *Psychoanalysis and religion*. New York: Bantam.

Gerth, H. H., & Mills, C. W. (1953). *Character and social structure: The psychology of social institutions*. New York: Harcourt, Brace.

Glassner, B., & Freedman, J. A. (1979). *Clinical sociology*. New York: Longman.

Goffman, E. (1959). *The presentation of self in everyday life*. New York: Doubleday.

Goode, E. (1968). Class styles of religious sociation. *British Journal of Sociology, 19,* 1–16.

Hall, C. M. (1981). *Individual and society*. Boonsboro, MD: Antietam Press.

Hall, C. M. (1986a). Crisis as opportunity for spiritual growth. *Journal of Religion and Health, 25,* 8–17.

Hall, C. M. (1986b). Cosmology and therapy. *Journal of Religion and Health, 25,* 254–263.

Hall, C. M. (1990a). Identity empowerment through clinical sociology. *Clinical Sociology Review, 8,* 69–86.

Hall, C. M. (1990b). *Women and identity: Value choices in a changing world*. New York: Hemisphere.

Hall, C. M. (1991). Clinical sociology and religion. *Clinical Sociology Review, 9,* 48–58.

Hammond, P. E. (1992). *Religion and personal autonomy: The third disestablishment in America*. Columbia, SC: University of South Carolina Press.

Haney, E. H. (1989). *Vision and struggle: Meditations on feminist spirituality and politics*. Portland, ME: Astarte Shell.

Haught, J. F. (1984). *The cosmic adventure: Science, religion and the quest for purpose*. New York: Paulist Press.

Hechter, M., Nadel, L., & Michod, R. E. (Eds.). (1993). *The origin of values*. New York: Aldine de Gruyter.

Herberg, W. (1955). *Protestant–Catholic–Jew*. New York: Doubleday.

Hess, D. J. (1991). *Spirits and scientists: Ideology, spiritism, and Brazilian culture*. University Park. PA: Pennsylvania State University Press.

Hunsberger, B. (1985). Life satisfaction and religion: A reanalysis. *Social Forces, 57,* 636–643.

Hussain, F. (Ed.). (1984). *Muslim women*. New York: St. Martin's Press.

James, W. (1969). *The varieties of religious experience*. New York: Collier.

Johnson, M. A. (1973). Family life and religious commitment. *Review of Religious Research, 14,* 144–150.

Jung, C. G. (1933). *Modern man in search of a soul*. New York: Harcourt, Brace and World.

Kaufman, G. D. (1993). *In face of mystery: A constructive theology*. Cambridge, MA: Harvard University Press.

Kosmin, B. A., & Lachman, S. P. (1993). *One nation under God: Religion in contemporary American society*. New York: Harmony.

Lenski, G. (1961). *The religious factor*. Garden City, NY: Doubleday.

Lerner, G. (1986). *The creation of patriarchy*. New York: Oxford University Press.

Lorentzen, R. (1991). *Women in the sanctuary movement*. Philadelphia: Temple University Press.

Luckmann, T. (1967). *The invisible religion.* New York: Macmillan.

Macionis, J. J., & Benokraitis, N. V. (Eds.). (1995). *Seeing ourselves: Classic, contemporary, and cross–cultural readings in sociology* (3d ed.). Englewood Cliffs, NJ: Prentice Hall.

Malony, H. N., & Southard, S. (Eds.). (1992). *Handbook of religious conversion.* Birmingham, AL: Religious Education Press.

Manuel, F. E., & Manuel, F. P. (1979). *Utopian thought in the western world.* Cambridge, MA: Harvard University Press.

Martin, D. (1990). *Tongues of fire: The explosion of Protestantism in Latin America.* Oxford, U.K.: Basil Blackwell.

Marty, M. E., & Appleby, R. S. (1991). *Fundamentalisms observed.* Chicago: University of Chicago Press.

McGuire, M. B. (1994). *Religion: The social context.* Belmont, CA: Wadsworth.

McNamara, P. H. (1992). *Conscience first, tradition second: A study of young American Catholics.* Albany, NY: State University of New York Press.

Mead, G. H. (1934). *Mind, self and society.* Chicago: University of Chicago Press.

Mol, H. (Ed.). (1978). *Identity and religion.* Beverly Hills, CA: Sage.

Ohnuki–Tierney, E. (1993). *Rice as self: Japanese identities through time.* Princeton, NJ: Princeton University Press.

Pargament, K. I., Kennell, J., Hathaway, W., Grevengoed, N., Newman, J., & Jones, W. (1988). Religion and the problem–solving process: three styles of coping. *Journal for the Scientific Study of Religion, 27,* 90–104.

Pollner, M. (1989). Divine relations, social relations, and well–being. *Journal of Health and Social Behavior, 30,* 92–104.

Poloma, M. M., & Gallup, G. H., Jr. (1991). *Varieties of prayer: A survey report.* Philadelphia: Trinity Press International.

Progoff, I. (1985). *Jung's psychology and its social meaning.* New York: Dialogue House.

Rambo, L. R. (1993). *Understanding religious conversion.* New Haven, CT: Yale University Press.

Randour, M. L. (Ed.). (1993). *Exploring sacred landscapes: Religious and spiritual experiences in psychotherapy.* New York: Columbia University Press.

Roof, W. C. (1992). *A generation of seekers: The spiritual journeys of the baby boom generation.* New York: Harper Collins.

Ryan, B. (1992). *Feminism and the women's movement: Dynamics of change in social movement ideology and activism.* New York: Routledge.

Schumaker, J. (Ed.). (1992). *Religion and mental health.* New York: Oxford University Press.

Smith, C. (1991). *The emergence of liberation theology: Radical religion and social movement theory.* Chicago: University of Chicago Press.

Smith, D. E. (1987). *The everyday world as problematic.* Toronto: University of Toronto Press.

Spretnak, C. (Ed.). (1982). *The politics of women's spirituality.* New York: Doubleday.

Stark, R., & Bainbridge, W. S. (1985). *The future of religion: Secularization, revival and cult formation.* Berkeley, CA: University of California Press.

Stark, R., & Glock, C. Y. (1968). *American piety: The nature of religious commitment.* Berkeley, CA: University of California Press.

Stoltenberg, J. (1989). *Refusing to be a man: Essays on sex and justice*. Portland, OR: Breitenbush.

Strunk, O., Jr. (1979). The world view factor in psychotherapy. *Journal of Religion and Health, 18,* 192–196.

Teilhard de Chardin, P. (1965). *The phenomenon of man*. New York: Harper and Row.

Tillich, P. (1952). *The courage to be*. New Haven: Yale University Press.

Van Zandt, D. E. (1991). *Living in the children of God*. Princeton, NJ: Princeton University Press.

Warner, R. S. (1993). Work in progress toward a new paradigm for the sociology of religion in the United States. *American Journal of Sociology, 98,* 1044–1093.

Weber, M. (1958). *The Protestant ethic and the spirit of capitalism*. New York: Charles Scribner's Sons.

Wilson, J. M. (1986). *Black messiahs and Uncle Toms: Social and literary manipulations of a religious myth*. University Park, PA: Pennsylvania State University Press.

Wuthnow, R. (1991). *Acts of compassion: Helping others and helping ourselves*. Princeton, NJ: Princeton University Press.

Wuthnow, R. (1992). *Rediscovering the sacred: Perspectives on religion in contemporary society*. Grand Rapids, MI: William B. Eerdmans.

Yinger, J. M. (1957). *Religion, society, and the individual*. New York: Macmillan.

Appendix

Identity Empowerment Theory

This book is based on a specific clinical sociological theory—identity empowerment theory—that the author has researched, developed, and applied in her practice of individual and family therapy throughout the past 25 years (Hall, 1990a). It is postulated here that broad sociological perspectives such as those used in identity empowerment theory can extend and enrich conventional intrapsychic or interpersonal frames of reference (Clark, 1990; Glassner & Freedman, 1979).

Clinical sociology is a relatively new discipline, which focuses on the influence of social contexts on behavior, as well as on the significance of interdependency for understanding behavior (Clark, 1990). Identity empowerment theory emphasizes particularly the influence of value choices on all kinds of interpersonal and social negotiations, and outlines some of the predictable, constructive consequences that result from strengthening identity through effective clinical interventions and behavior changes, with reference to basic social institutions such as families and religions (Hall, 1986b, 1990a, 1991).

Identity empowerment theory consists of 10 interrelated concepts that describe, and to a certain extent explain, key social processes and social structures within and between complex human dependencies. The concepts of identity empowerment theory are: self, dyad, triad, family, religion, definition of the situation, reference group, class, culture, and society. These concepts represent a sequence of ever-increasing social spheres of interaction, as well as different levels of individual and social awareness of their influence. The 10 basic concepts of identity empowerment theory also shift its central focus from interpersonal, private, or microsociological milieus to broad, public, or macrosociological domains.

Identity is essentially an experiential or perceived bond or bridge between the self and different levels of social organization. The concepts of identity empowerment theory represent critical situational or structural influences on self, which can also be thought of as intervening variables when considering the relationship between self and society from objective, social systems, or scientific viewpoints. Empowerment describes optimal therapeutic or growth processes that result from clinical or social exchanges, whereby identity is strengthened and individuals become more effective in their personal, professional, and political negotiations with others.

Identity empowerment theory can be applied to individuals and their social processes or social structures at all levels of micro- and macroanalysis: interpersonal, family, religious, gender, community, social class, race, ethnic group, political, social movement, societal, historical, and evolutionary. Identity empowerment theory also suggests directions for effective clinical interventions, as well as provides broad contexts for understanding varied patterns of interaction. In these respects identity empowerment theory gives both depth and scope to varied planning activities, including therapeutic strategies and crisis resolutions.

One way to understand this range of potential uses of identity empowerment theory, together with specific applications to the substantive theme of identity and religion, is to examine each of the 10 basic concepts more closely. However, each of these 10 concepts has systems relationships with the other 9; to understand any one concept of identity empowerment theory as fully as possible, One must consider it in the context of all of the others.

SELF

Self can be thought of as the innermost part of individual being. Self is moral agency and the source of value choices and integrity. Self also initiates and results from presentations of individuality to others (Goffman, 1959). Optimally, people have deep-seated values and beliefs that make up the core of self, as well as more peripheral values and beliefs that change and shift more easily (Bowen, 1978).

Self may also be thought of as a conceptualization of perceptions of relationships with others (Cooley, 1964; Mead, 1934). Personal character is largely made up of expressions of negotiable and nonnegotiable values, which result from socialization or resocialization.

To empower the self, and thus change behavior effectively, a precondition of fairly high levels of self-awareness and self-knowledge must be achieved. For example, people can find out what their most important priorities and preferences are by examining the ways they interact with intimate others and authority figures. This becomes a base of self-knowledge from which other changes can be made.

People are essentially their successful or failed expressions of integrity, their compromises, and their successes or failures as historical actors. Because human beings' perspectives of self and the world may be either relatively restrictive or expansive, optimally clinical interventions open up individuals' habitual frames of reference for assessing their particular situations and opportunities.

Self is both the beginning point and the end result of individual thoughts, beliefs, and actions. People automatically increase their responsibilities when they know who they are, and when they see and do whatever is possible for them to make constructive contributions to society. Even though they may try to delegate many responsibilities to others, they cannot escape the necessity of making value choices in all the situations in which they find themselves.

DYAD

Although some social scientists consider dyads, or two-person relationships, to be basic units of social interaction, dyads are intrinsically unstable and need to be considered in contexts of more complex relationship systems, such as families or social classes. In fact, this very property, the inherent precariousness of dyads, makes them relatively unsatisfactory units of analysis for understanding human behavior.

Particular exchanges and transactions are integral parts of broad social processes and structures, so that the specific value choices of participants in dyads influence and are influenced by broad patterns of superordination, subordination, and other kinds of dependencies and power relations. Furthermore, because dyads are frequently volatile, they may not endure through long periods of time, and are therefore necessarily replaced by other dyads or triads.

TRIAD

A triad is a three-person relationship. In contrast to a dyad, a triad is relatively stable and therefore can more effectively serve as a basic unit of any group, social class, or social organization. Because of the omnipresence of latent or active triads in relationship systems, all kinds of social groupings can be analyzed in terms of triadic interaction.

One member of a triad generally holds an outsider position in relation to either the closeness or the reciprocal animosity of the remaining twosome. However, the dynamics of triads shift easily; and as patterns of togetherness or conflict change, outsiders may become insiders, and insiders may become outsiders. In most situations, the outsider position in triads is more autonomous, and therefore stronger, than either of the insider positions.

A triad forms when the level of anxiety in a dyad is sufficiently high that a third person is drawn into the dyad to stabilize the relationship and lower the anxiety. If one person leaves a triad, the remaining dyad may pull a substitute third party into the relationship, thus perpetuating the triad. Furthermore, whenever a dyad has high levels of anxiety or stress, it is inevitable that a third party is drawn into the twosome.

Because triads are necessarily closely interrelated with other triads, any kind of group or larger social form can be understood in terms of being a system of complex interlocking triads. Thus, a triad is a basic unit of organization, and triads affect the behavior of groups and societies as well as of individuals.

FAMILY

Families are defined as the most intense emotional systems that exist, whose memberships are based on kin relations or contractual agreements. Families are also the most closely interdependent lifelong groups to which individuals belong.

Most people have active or dormant family relationships, and optimally these bonds are experienced as meaningful. However, other kinds of support groups and networks may serve many of the same functions as families, especially if these groups develop the equivalent of intergenerational contacts through time. Similarly, long-standing friendships may become integrated into family emotional systems, with the result that close friends may resemble relatives with respect to the impact of their influences on individuals' behavior.

Both traditional and nontraditional families are emotional systems, although the players in these different groupings and their patterns of interaction may vary considerably. The most important property of families for functioning purposes is that they should be open rather than closed relationship systems. Thus family members can be relatively autonomous, with flexible behavior patterns that are markedly less repetitive and less symptomatic than behavior patterns in closed relationship systems.

RELIGION

For the purposes of conceptualizing identity empowerment, religions here are defined broadly as belief systems about visible and invisible realities that are held to be sacred. The characteristics of religion are universalist rather than particular, and it is these more general kinds of properties that need to be considered carefully in clinical work (Hall, 1991). Religions include people's deepest values, beliefs, and assumptions about supernatural and natural influences, which may be expressed in a wide variety of denominational or sectarian forms. Furthermore, evolutionary perspectives can be useful frames of reference for determining particular patterns in religious development (Durkheim, 1915).

Traditional religious beliefs are influenced by secularization and the presence of increasing numbers of more varied religions, with the result that new kinds of religious expressions emerge. Nevertheless, however religions change, they continue to be the most significant sources of values and beliefs for many people, in that both traditional and emergent religious forms and processes provide purposes and directions for everyday behavior (Warner, 1993). Furthermore, religions sacralize certain secular values and beliefs, so that ideals and optimal conditions become cherished goals for human endeavors, as well as signifiers of social status (Goode, 1968).

DEFINITION OF THE SITUATION

Definitions of life situations are crucial subjective links between self-understanding and perceptions of society. However, these subjective views of social realities result as much from holding particular beliefs and values as from the empirical dimensions of given situations. Effective clinical work heightens clients' awareness about the role their subjective understanding plays in determining their behavior, as well as assists in formulating necessary redefinitions of situations so as to change problematic behavior.

Definitions and redefinitions of situations are based on individual and social value choices. Thus, reality is a social construction that may be directly related to religious or secular beliefs (Berger & Luckmann, 1967). Clinical intervention helps clients expand their perceptions and understanding of life situations through internalization of new values or activation of dormant ones. These values orient actions and predispose behavior toward specific outcomes, and beliefs about self and reality are particularly influential motivating forces for bringing about significant behavioral consequences. Thus identity empowerment results from clients' self-conscious, deliberate redefinitions of significant aspects of their individual and social living situations (Hunsberger, 1985).

REFERENCE GROUP

Reference groups may be associated with either ascribed or achieved characteristics. Ascribed reference groups include sex, race, and ethnicity, whereas achieved reference groups include occupations, professions, and religious denominations (Collins, 1990). People are born into ascribed reference groups, whereas they choose to belong to their achieved reference groups. A reference group may be a group to which people actually belong or a group to which they aspire to belong. The intensity of their senses of belonging to specific groups and their resulting identifications with these groups have special meaning to individuals and may play crucial roles in either increasing or decreasing their social mobility.

Thus behavior is strongly influenced by people's senses of belonging to particular reference groups, whether or not they actually belong to these groups. Clinical interventions heighten clients' awareness of the reference group commitments they have already made, as well as of those they would like to make.

CLASS

Individual behavior is anchored in social classes. Social classes may be based on economic assets, age, gender, sexual orientation, race, ethnicity, or age, even though they are not formally organized. Many people are unaware of having any class memberships, even though all members of a given population may be categorized by others as belonging to specific social classes.

In spite of this general lack of recognition, class membership frequently has a strong influence on behavior. In fact, many value choices reflect particular class memberships, in that these choices express specific class cultures. Ideally, clinical interventions help clients understand the influences of their class memberships on their behavior. Furthermore, clinical discussions, decision making, and resulting actions can decrease or neutralize some social class influences on individual and social behavior, and this increased autonomy may result in increased social mobility.

CULTURE

Culture consists of the sum total of a society's majority and minority group values. Cultures are frequently polarized by traditional and modern values, by individual-oriented or collectivity-oriented values, or by constructive or destructive values. In addition, mainstream values have strong influences on each person's behavior, even if these individuals are members of minority groups.

Religions are at the core of cultures, but both religious and secular values are expressed in any given culture. Necessary value negotiations with others can occur only through the filters of dominant cultural values, which shape all individual and social concerns or issues. Therefore, because culture is such a significant influence on behavior, when cultural values change quickly or are ambiguous, individual actions may be disoriented (Durkheim, 1951).

SOCIETY

Society is the most comprehensive social structure with which an individual identifies, and this kind of identification is necessary for survival, as well as for the enhancement of specific qualities of social life (Durkheim, 1951). Concepts of society depend on shared understanding of history, evolution, and the universe, and suggest the broadest contexts of being human (Cooley, 1964).

World views influence behavior, and religions are frequently important sources of world views (Strunk, 1979). Clinical discussions can enhance clients' abilities to compare their beliefs about society with empirical realities, so that clients can make more enlightened choices of values (Smith, 1987). It is by giving attention to this broadest social context that identity empowerment is achieved, when clinicians are able to strengthen their clients' capacities to articulate their most meaningful and most representative views of themselves, the world, and the universe (Hall, 1990a).

Therefore, maintaining a clinical focus on clients' concepts of society can expand their awareness of their identities and action possibilities. When clinicians encourage their clients to place themselves in the context of societies, history, or evolution, clients' abilities to transcend the restrictions of their actual living conditions are enhanced. Thus greater self-knowledge and identity empowerment are achieved through applying these kinds of comprehensive perspectives to clients' experiences, which necessarily include making references to religions and other moral views of the universe (Hall, 1986a; Pollner, 1989; Teilhard de Chardin, 1965).

Index